Get **more** out of libraries

Please return or renew this item by the last date shown.
You can renew online at www.hants.gov.uk/library
Or by phoning 0845 603 5631

Hampshire
County Council

385.509428

RAILWAY & SOCIETY

First published in 1992
by the Railway & Canal Historical Society
Registered office: Fron Fawnog, Hafod Road, Gwernymynydd, Mold, Clwyd CH7 5JS
Registered charity no.256047

ISBN 0 901461 15 6

Designed and typeset by
Malcolm Preskett and Carol Davie
Printed in England by
Hobbs the Printers of Southampton

FRONT COVER
Conisbrough Viaduct where the Dearne Valley Railway
crossed the Don Valley (photo D. Rogerson & P. Baker)

Inset: Sebastian Meyer *c.*1906 (photo Collection G. Sellers)
(see illustration no. 13)

BACK COVER
A sentinel rail car at Haxey Junction
on the Axholme Joint Railway.
(photo G. J. Aston)

Contents

Foreword

THE WRITING of railway history has itself a history almost as long as that of the railways for what occurred yesterday has become history today. Aspects which have been dealt with are indeed numerous – mechanical history of locomotives and other rolling stock; the civil engineering involved in construction of the lines; the evolution of train services and traffic; and the wheeling and dealing involved in the financing of lines.

But there would have been no railway history because there would have been no railways without the efforts of individuals and railway history must include studies of personalities. All too often these have been of engineers and all too infrequently of entrepreneurs and managers, though there have been some excellent recent studies. But it has been the Captain Mark Huish's, of the large companies such as the London & North Western, that have attracted the attention of historians. But the British railway system included many miles of minor and often independent lines. Studies of those who promoted, built and managed these companies are therefore of very great value.

Dr Barnett has chosen as his subject Sebastian Meyer, who was involved in the creation and operation of a number of minor and secondary lines in the North East of England, comparing him with the much better known southern entrepreneur, Colonel Stephens.

Among the dozen or so light railways promoted by Meyer were the Dearne Valley, Isle of Axholme, North Lindsey and North Sunderland. Some were successful, and some still survive, but others were not and are now just a memory in the railway history of the North East.

Dr Barnett reveals the entrepreneurial circles within which Meyer moved; how they obtained their finances and necessary Acts and Light Railway Orders; their often stormy relations with the larger railway companies; and the frequent uphill struggles to keep their companies out of bankruptcy. But he does more, Meyer was a man of wide interests, Director of a coal mine, an oil factory and the Wensleydale Pure Milk Society; Alderman of the City of York; member of the Society of Friends: a keen amateur musician and a family man. He emerges from these pages as a rounded character.

And we also get a picture of the lines themselves, which with very few exceptions have passed into history. Here is a splendid picture based on much original research of railway development in the North East and of life in York.

H.P. White, MA MCIT FRSA
Emeritus Professor, University of Salford and Past President
of the Railway & Canal Historical Society.

Introduction

WRITING accurate railway history is a difficult and expensive pastime. It is difficult because it is now impossible to obtain complete evidence of all the facts. Minutes of the principal railway companies remain, but these vary greatly in their helpfulness. Some are minutely detailed (excuse the pun), while others are no more than an *aide memoire* for the directors. In some cases items well known to the Board are not even recorded, to the annoyance of the later historian. One learns that 'a letter was read from the Solicitor', but there is no means of knowing its contents or importance. Deductions have to be made and, inevitably, if further research material comes to light, they may be proved wrong.

Salvage drives of two major wars have led to the destruction of many valuable records. The writer must not be too disappointed to receive replies saying 'unfortunately the majority of our earlier files were destroyed when we left our old office'.

It is expensive, especially for the provincial author, as all the railway company papers are kept in the Public Record Office at Kew (until fairly recently the records of the North Eastern Railway Company were available in York). This is not to say there is not a wealth of material to be consulted locally. The National Railway Museum, York has extensive collections of contemporary railway periodicals, timetables, etc. The County Record Offices hold the Deposited Plans and Bills for all railways built or proposed in their area and many of them have a full set of Local and Personal Acts of Parliament. District Libraries have files of local newspapers, a valuable source of information, but one which requires some degree of caution in its use. Some of them, unfortunately, are on undecipherable microfilm. Details of the sources used are given in the Acknowledgements.

Careful consideration has been given to the subject of references. As nearly all the statements in the book are factual, inclusion of references would almost double its length and would be tedious for the majority of readers. It has therefore been reluctantly decided to omit all but the most important.

As far as possible the author has endeavoured not to duplicate what has already been published on the various railways covered herein. For further details the reader is referred to the company histories listed in the Bibliography. However, not all of the works mentioned can be equally recommended. All prices are quoted in pounds, shillings and pence current at the time to which they refer.

ACKNOWLEDGEMENTS

I AM INDEBTED to many public bodies whose staffs have willingly assisted me. Foremost the Public Record Office, Kew, and the Library of the National Railway Museum, York. I have been helped by many County Record Offices, including Northumberland, North Yorkshire, West Yorkshire (now West Yorkshire Archives Service in Wakefield and Leeds), Lincolnshire and Greater London. I have visited libraries in Northallerton, York, Leeds, Doncaster, Goole and Scunthorpe, where I have consulted local newspapers. The Central Libraries of Newcastle-upon-Tyne and Hull have sent useful cuttings. The Institute of Civil Engineers has provided valuable potted biographies of Messrs Mammatt and Kay and the Institute of Bankers has answered my queries. I thank the Editor of the *Railway Observer* for permission to use extracts from that magazine. The Religious Society of Friends has sent me a copy of Sebastian Meyer's obituary which appeared in *Friends*. I have been assisted by the British Railways' Solicitor, Paddington and by the Librarian, Brunel University.

On a more personal note, I have been greatly helped on family matters by the late Philip F. Meyer, Sebastian's grandson, and by Mr G. Sellers. The former willingly gave me great assistance in spite of a very distressing illness. Mr R. S. Mortimer has made available to me the records of the York Monthly Meeting in the Brotherton Library, University of Leeds. I am grateful to Mr J. F. Goodchild, who has allowed me to use his Charlesworth papers.

Mr Richard Dean has drawn the maps from drafts by Mr H. Keyte. I have been helped by Messrs J. Edgington, K. Hoole, D. Jackson, H. Murray, J. Petrie, K. P. Plant, J. Howard Turner, of Sheffield, and A. Watts.

Thanks are also due to members of the Railway & Canal Historical Society for their assistance in the production of this book, namely, Grahame Boyes, Tony Jervis, Michael Messenger, Malcolm Preskett, Silvia Rymel and Pat White. Gordon Green, Brian Hinchliffe and Trevor Lodge have read my poor typing, made necessary amendments and provided me with much additional information. Once again I am indebted to Trevor for his expert photography.

Finally my sincere apologies to anyone who may have been inadvertently omitted.

CHAPTER ONE

Early days

MOST RAILWAY ENTHUSIASTS have heard of Lt-Colonel Holman Fred Stephens (1868–1931) who has been named 'The Light Railway King'. An equally able and versatile, but perhaps not so flamboyant character, resided in the North of England at about the same period. This was Sebastian William Meyer of York. The two men were the leading promoters of light and minor lines from the end of the last century to the commencement of World War I, when the railways of this country were at the zenith of their extent and prosperity. In some respects they were the opposite in character. Meyer was a pacifist, while Stephens served in the First World War in the Royal Engineers. Stephens was first an engineer – he was a Member of the Institution of Civil Engineers – who later came to management; Meyer was essentially an entrepreneur, although without formal training he styled himself in later life 'Engineer'. Stephens, with some notable exceptions, concentrated on passenger carrying lines, while Meyer was chiefly interested in goods traffic. Kidner, in his *The Light Railways of Britain*, states that Stephens 'will always be remembered for his lavish purchases of superannuated main-line rolling stock for his lines'. Meyer on the other hand, was practical and economical in his investment. Some of Stephens' railways were taken over by the Great Western Railway or were nationalised, perhaps unwillingly. Meyer's railways were taken over more quickly. Unfortunately none of Meyer's has been acquired by a Preservation Society.

It is possible that the two men may have met, as Meyer is known to have frequently attended meetings of the Association of Smaller Railway Companies and it would be interesting to speculate on their conversation.

Sebastian William Meyer was born in London on 10 April 1856. The family was originally German, but moved in the eighteenth century to Strasbourg in Alsace (at that time, as now, in France). They were gifted musicians, many of them professionals. Of these Sebastian's direct ancestor, Philip John (the English spelling is used) went to Paris, but was unable to settle there and migrated to London in 1768, bringing with him his young son, aged two years and of the same name. This Meyer became a naturalised British citizen by Act of Parliament. He later taught the harp to Queen Adelaide, Consort of King William IV.

His son was Sebastian Louis John Meyer (Sebastian became a family name, probably from admiration of the music of Johann Sebastian Bach). He was also musical, but by profession was a wholesale provision merchant, in particular of dairy produce (appropriately as *Meier* is German for dairy farmer). He died from typhoid fever in 1866, leaving his widow with six young children of whom Sebastian was the second eldest.

The boy also caught the disease, but recovered. He was educated at the North London Collegiate School, Kentish Town. He left at the early age of twelve years, as he had to help his mother to support the rest of the family. He thus received only scanty schooling. In spite of this, in later life he travelled extensively. He was something of a linguist, but, as he was self-taught, he had great difficulty in understanding and making himself understood on his journeys.

He first obtained a position as office-boy with

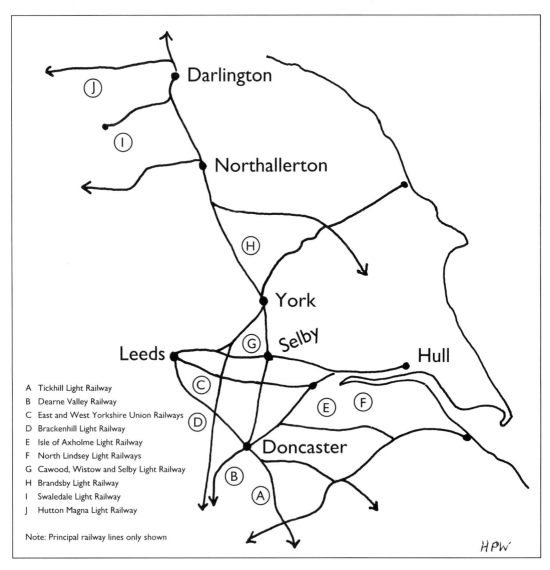

A Tickhill Light Railway
B Dearne Valley Railway
C East and West Yorkshire Union Railways
D Brackenhill Light Railway
E Isle of Axholme Light Railway
F North Lindsey Light Railways
G Cawood, Wistow and Selby Light Railway
H Brandsby Light Railway
I Swaledale Light Railway
J Hutton Magna Light Railway

Note: Principal railway lines only shown

1. Map showing the railways for which Sebastian Meyer was engineer.

a firm of solicitors. At the age of seventeen he became a junior clerk in the office of Frederick Saunders, the Secretary of the Great Western Railway at Paddington. The story goes that two lads were set the task of copying an article from *The Times*. The other unfortunate boy made one mistake. Sebastian, in spite of his lack of education, made none. So he was awarded the job. He stayed at Paddington for eight years.

In 1881, a year after its incorporation, Meyer became Assistant Secretary to the Hull, Barnsley & West Riding Junction Railway & Dock Company*. For almost the rest of his life he lived in the North of England. The musical talent of the family was inherited and about this time he composed the words and music of a part-song entitled 'A Holiday Reminiscence', which he dedicated to the Hull & Barnsley Railway Choral Association.

Over the years Meyer became interested in a dozen railways in the North East of England. The most important of these were the East & West Yorkshire Union Railways (note the plural is used in several of the titles of the railways with which Meyer was associated), the North Lindsey Light, and the Dearne Valley. The first two of these were absorbed into the London & North Eastern Railway and the last, eventually, into the London Midland & Scottish, becoming important feeders to the main lines until alterations in the pattern of industry led to closures in whole or part. The Goole & Marshland and the Isle of Axholme were acquired jointly by the North Eastern and the Lancashire & Yorkshire. The Tickhill Light Railway was purchased by the Great Northern. These last three became important pawns in the railway politics of South Yorkshire. The Cawood, Wistow & Selby and the Brackenhill fell fairly early into the hands of the NER. The North Sunderland, after a long but precarious existence, was in the end managed by the LNER and later by British Railways. His last projects, the Brandsby, the Swaledale and the Hutton Magna Light Railways, never got off the ground. The first two were approved by the Light Railway Commissioners and the Hutton Magna managed to obtain its Light Railway Order from the Board of Trade. No doubt they were casualties of the First World War.

In addition to his railway activities, Meyer took a major interest in the municipal affairs of his adopted city of York. He became a member of the Society of Friends (Quakers) and was for many years a leader of the York Monthly Meeting. He was a Director of a coal mine situated between Wakefield and Leeds and the founder of an oil factory in the same area. He was one of the original Directors of the Wensleydale Pure Milk Society, Northallerton, one of the first dairies to pasteurise and bottle milk.

---

* At this time this was the correct title of the railway company.
It officially became the Hull & Barnsley Railway by Act of 1905.
For convenience the shorter and better known title is used in this book.

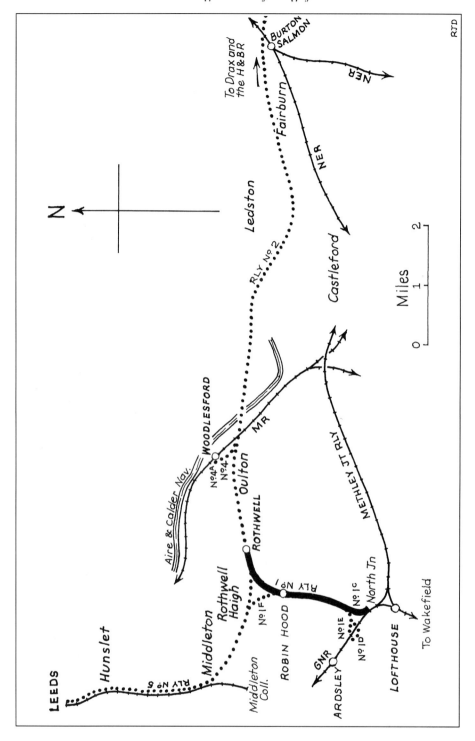

RJD

2. The East & West Yorkshire Union Railways – Railway No. 1.

CHAPTER TWO

The East & West Yorkshire Union Railways

THE East & West Yorkshire Union Railways Company (like the Cambrian and a few other railways, the Company always used the plural) was originally promoted by certain coal owners and landowners of West Yorkshire. They were dissatisfied with the transport facilities between their district and the port of Hull provided by the North Eastern Railway and the Aire & Calder Navigation. The Bill, submitted to Parliament in 1881, included a main line from junctions with the Great Northern near Ardsley and at Lofthouse to a junction with the main line of the Hull & Barnsley, which had only been authorised a year earlier, near Drax. There were to be junctions with the Midland at Woodlesford and with the NER at Burton Salmon. Running powers were sought over the GNR to Ardsley station and to Wakefield, over the MR to Woodlesford and over the H&BR and/or the NER.

The House of Commons Select Committee struck out the southern connection at Lofthouse, the junction with the Midland at Woodlesford and with the NER at Burton Salmon. The House of Lords Committee did not like what was left and decided the 'preamble was not proved'.

Nothing daunted, the promoters deposited even more ambitious plans in the ensuing Session of 1882–3. The main line was much as before, but an important branch was added from Rothwell to terminate in a central position in Leeds, near Leeds Bridge. The connection at Woodlesford was now only to the sidings of the Midland. It was agreed that the E&WYUR would purchase about two miles of the historic Middleton Railway at Leeds, that it would build a passenger station near Middleton

Broom Pit and provide at least two passenger trains a day. The Middleton would have running powers, and junctions would be included, so that it could continue to supply coal to Meadow Lane Gas Works and to the Leeds Ironworks.

After Agreements had been made with the GNR with regard to the junctions at Ardsley and Lofthouse, that Company no longer opposed and the opposition of the NER broke down. The new railway was welcomed by the infant H&BR. Its Chairman said that 'the first Bill was from nowhere to nowhere'. He continued 'if it gets into hostile hands, it would be the means undoubtedly of diverting a very considerable amount of traffic from the Hull and Barnsley'. He reported that negotiations with the promoters of the E&WYUR were taking place and that 'an Agreement cannot but be advantageous'. This was completed on 1 May 1883.

The Act was duly passed in August 1883. It incorporated the Company, with a capital of £1,200,000 in £10 shares and borrowing powers of £400,000. Traffic and Working Agreements could be made with the H&BR and there was to be a joint station at Drax. The E&WYUR had running powers to that station and the H&BR had reciprocal powers over the whole of the E&WYUR. To show the hopes of the new Company, its Seal included the Coats of Arms of the Cities of Leeds and Hull.

The first Directors of the new Company were Lord Beaumont of Carlton Towers, who was also a Director of the H&BR; Joseph and Charles Ernest Charlesworth of Messrs J. & J. Charlesworth Limited; Edward Bower of E. Bower & Son of Fenchurch Street, London; and Samson Fox,

Managing Director of the Leeds Forge Company. Later in the year, Henry Ellis of Birkin, a subscriber, wrote to say that he would be willing to become a Director and take a share in the liabilities of the Company. He took his seat in October. The Engineers were Malcolm Paterson of Dewsbury and Isaac White of Leeds. George Hopkins was Consulting Engineer. T. G. Teale was appointed Solicitor and *pro tem* Secretary.

Joseph Charlesworth was elected Chairman. The Charlesworth family had been colliery proprietors from early in the nineteenth century. They owned Robin Hood colliery which, before the coming of the E&WYUR, had been connected to the GNR by a tramway (abandoned in 1896); Rothwell Haigh, or Beeston Pit, connected to the MR by a rope-worked incline down to Stourton; Rothwell, or Rose Pit; and the Newmarket Collieries joined to the Aire & Calder Navigation by a tramway, built as early as 1836 on land leased from the Calverley family.

Early in December 1883, the Acting Secretary reported that Sebastian Meyer, the Assistant Secretary of the H&BR, had applied for the position of Secretary to the Company. Teale was instructed to write to him and, at an interview before the Board on 27 December, Meyer was appointed at a salary of £300 per annum, with three months notice on either side. This may be described as his first step towards becoming the successful railway entrepreneur which he eventually became.

A letter from the Secretary of the H&BR, which was now in some financial difficulty, was received in April 1884, stating that his Company would postpone all existing liabilities and enter upon no fresh obligations until after the completion of their railway between Hull and Cudworth, and of their Alexandra Dock at Hull.

The Chairman of the E&WYUR, no doubt acting on the advice of his new Secretary, approached Henry Lambert, at that time Goods Manager of the Great Western Railway, with a view to arranging Agreements with the GNR. This was accomplished in November. About this time, Lord Beaumont resigned from the Board; possibly he felt that he could serve no useful purpose in trying

3. Robin Hood station in June 1963 looking north. *Collection D. Thompson*

to represent two companies. T. Bower of Messrs T. & R. W. Bower, Allerton Main Colliery, was elected in his place.

In the following year, the offices of the Company were moved to temporary premises at the address of Mammatt & White, 1 Albion Place, Leeds. Further negotiations were conducted by Lambert and Meyer with the GNR and the H&BR, but they were unable to reach satisfactory conclusions.

In June 1886 the Company obtained its second Act which included alterations to the connecting lines at Ardsley and Lofthouse in accordance with Agreements it had made with the GNR in 1883.

An important clause in the Act authorised a south to west curve from near Lofthouse to near Robin Hood which would allow through running to Leeds. The NER had petitioned against the Bill, alleging that the H&BR was in no position to work the E&WYUR, in view of its commitments to other railways. Meyer now reported that he had been able to come to an arrangement with the H&BR for a grant of Running Powers over that line to places west of the River Hull and to Sculcoates. An Agreement was also reached with the GNR that that Company would work the E&WYUR from Leeds to Ardsley but not to Drax. The vacancy on the Board caused by the resignation of Ellis was filled by A. T. Lawson.

All this time, nothing had been done towards raising the capital or constructing the line, so the Directors decided to issue a prospectus which appeared in October 1887. It listed the Directors and stated the authorised capital. Part of the Middleton Railway was to be purchased. There were to be stations at Leeds Bridge, Rothwell, Robin Hood, Oulton, Ledston (for Castleford), Fairburn, Birkin, Gateforth, Burn, Camblesforth, and 'other intermediate places', and there was to be a branch to the Midland at Woodlesford. The total length was about 30 miles. Traffic could be forwarded to Bradford, Keighley, Barrow and Carlisle over the Midland, to Wakefield, Doncaster and London over the GNR and to Grimsby over the Manchester, Sheffield & Lincolnshire Railway. The Company had Running Powers to Alexandra Dock over the H&BR. A coloured map was included. Subscriptions were now invited.

At the end of the year, T. Bower resigned after a

very short stay on the Board. James Ashwin was appointed Chief Clerk at a salary of £100 per annum, while David Stewart Hartmann became Assistant Clerk at the smaller salary of £65 per annum. This is the first mention of Mr Hartmann who became associated with Meyer in many projects over a long period of time. His Christian names suggest Scottish connections but his surname has a Teutonic ring. At this time, 1887, he was 34 years of age.

On 17 February 1888 the tender of Whitaker Brothers for the construction of the railway from Lofthouse to Rothwell was accepted and Whitakers agreed to take £6,000 in fully paid-up shares towards their payment. At the General Meeting of the Company a few days later, Joseph Charlesworth, as Chairman, said that they might seem slow in promoting the railway but there had been many difficulties to contend with and they had not met with the support from the public they had expected. Enough capital had been raised to enable them to make a portion of the railway which he hoped would pay well. Meyer's salary of £300 a year was confirmed 'subject to such alteration as the Directors think fit'. It is hoped that 'such alteration' would be upward as he was already receiving that amount. The Company's offices were now moved to 11 Park Row, Leeds.

The Company obtained another Act in July, which stated that the railways between Ardsley and Leeds might be constituted as a separate company. It stated that the bridge over the Aire & Calder Navigation near Woodlesford, authorised in the 1883 Act, must be constructed as an opening bridge (the A&CN was a powerful organisation which hoped to turn its waterway into a ship canal), but the bridge did not need be worked as an opening bridge until all the other bridges over the Navigation had been similarly altered. Earlier the Navigation Company had withdrawn its opposition to the Bill when the above conditions had been agreed and it promised to pay £500 towards its cost on completion. It was also agreed that the bridges over the River Aire and over the Selby Canal, might be constructed as fixed bridges. An extension of time for the construction of the railway was granted.

At the half-yearly meeting of the Company in Leeds in October, according to the *Railway Times*, the Chairman was distinctly 'cagey' in his report, but the paper understood that £67,280 had been raised and £36,393 expended. Construction was well in hand. It was confirmed that the engineering work be planned by the firm of Mammatt & White.

This concern made Stanley Robert Kay their Superintending Engineer for the line, a position which he later held on the South Leeds Junction Railway and on the Newmarket Branch. He also laid out and was responsible for the Cawood, Wistow & Selby Light Railway. After 1899, as a partner in the firm, he was engaged as Chief Engineer for the Goole & Marshland and the Isle of Axholme Light Railways until they were taken over by the North Eastern and Lancashire & Yorkshire Railways in 1902. He was Engineer to the Dearne Valley Railway from 1899, and he prepared all the plans for, and was responsible for the construction of, this railway from its commencement until it, in turn, came under the control of the L&YR.

Charles E. Charlesworth took the Chair at the next half-yearly meeting and he said that he hoped to be sending colliery traffic over nearly the whole of the line before the next meeting. This was followed by a special meeting to support a Bill to allow the Company to abandon a small part of its line in Leeds. The shareholders were told that the H&BR Company was applying for powers to transfer to the NER. The E&WYUR Act of Incorporation had been obtained, partly on the evidence of the Chairman of the H&BR promising that his Company would send traffic over the E&WYUR. If the NER acquired the H&BR, that traffic would be diverted. The Directors had frequently approached the H&BR to get Agreements which would help the E&WYUR to raise the capital necessary to construct the whole of its line, but without success, although earlier the H&BR had promised to assist. The Directors had, therefore, reluctantly come to the conclusion that the H&BR could not, or would not, help them. The Bill would also reduce the amount of capital required. Negotiations with a view to extending to Hunslet were being carried out but there was no definite settlement at the moment.

The H&BR proposals for amalgamation were withdrawn from its Bill. The E&WYUR Act of 1889 authorised the proposed abandonment from Great Wilson Street to Hunslet Lane, Leeds. At the

second General Meeting of the year, with Joseph Charlesworth in the Chair once more, it was reported that the bulk of the present contract was finished. The Directors thought it inexpedient to abandon the major portion of the railway but the cut-off of the short extension to Hunslet Lane would allow them to reduce the capital powers to £900,000. Meanwhile the H&BR minuted that a proposed Working Agreement with the E&WYUR could not be entertained and, later, that no Agreement with the E&WYUR was possible at the present time.

At the February 1890 General Meeting, J. Charlesworth reported that a slip between Lingwell Gate and Robin Hood at Thorpe Lane had caused delay but he hoped the railway would be opened in the summer. The lines existing at present were contractor's lines. There would be a passenger station at Rothwell. This appears to be the first reference to the intention to run a passenger service, apart from the one agreed with the Middleton Colliery Company. He confirmed that the authorised capital was £900,000 but £632,000 was unissued. Bills were being prepared, one of which was for an extensive abandonment of the authorised main line. This indicates a rapid change of mind by the Board, as the Chairman had stated at the Autumn meeting that it was not advisable to shorten the railway, and the Bill had to be submitted to Parliament by the end of November. It was also proposed to alter the name of the Company but the author has been unable to discover what title was chosen and the matter seems to have been dropped. The second Bill was for an extension of time. The Bills appear to have been merged and the Act was passed in July 1890. It stated that the Company was proceeding with the construction of part of its line but that the estimated cost for the construction of the main line from Leeds to Drax was £636,825 (which bears a remarkable similarity to the unissued capital). The Agreement with the Middleton Company was cancelled. That Company had withdrawn their opposition to the Bill on payment to them of £3,500 but the Colliery was to purchase £3,500 shares in the Railway Company. This seems to be another way of saying that the Colliery was given £3,500 Railway shares as compensation. The Act again dramatically reduced the capital to £150,000

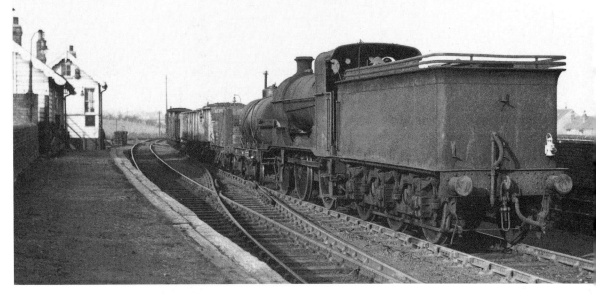

4. A Stourton–Ardsley coal train headed by ex-GNR class J6 0-6-0 No.64226 passes Robin Hood in March 1961. *P. Cookson*

with borrowing powers of £50,000.

In October, William Hargreaves, Coal Agent of Rothwell Haigh, was appointed a Director. Negotiations took place with the GNR with a view to that Company working the line and the following month it was reported that the permanent way was being laid and traffic was now passing on to the GNR, no doubt hauled by contractor's locomotives.

The year 1891 was an important one for the Company and for Meyer. The Railway was opened for goods and mineral traffic on 20 May. It was a single line with parts doubled. Robin Hood siding was opened on 25 May. In February, Philip Robert Meyer, Sebastian's younger brother, was appointed auditor at a fee of twenty guineas (£21.00) a year, a position which he retained until 1899. A month later, Sebastian became Secretary and General Manager at a salary of £400 per annum.

In the following year Isaac White was appointed a Director in place of Samson Fox and he resigned as Engineer. The Company again tried to raise further ordinary capital.

In 1893 John E. Mammatt became Engineer to the Company; on the face of it, a surprising appointment as Mammatt was primarily a mining engineer.

Meanwhile, events had been moving in another direction. In 1891/92 certain Leeds businessmen proposed to construct a railway from the E&WYUR at Rothwell to terminate near the Hunslet Lane goods station of the Midland in a central position in Leeds. They were unsuccessful in their application to Parliament but applied again in the next year. The South Leeds Junction Railway Company was incorporated in 1893, with a capital of £60,000 and borrowing powers of £20,000 to build a much curtailed line from Rothwell to finish on the south side of the Midland (but with no junction) near to the Leeds–Pontefract road. The Directors named in the Act were Alf Cooke, Charles Coghlan, Stanley Elmore and three others. The Company could make Working Agreements with the Midland and/or the E&WYUR and it obtained Running Powers over the latter. That Company was to work the line (although it had no locomotives), it was to receive the rates for carriage and pay tolls of between 4d and 9d per ton. It was rumoured that both the E&WYUR and the South Leeds Junction would be acquired by the Midland.

Returning to the E&WYUR, an Agreement was made in 1894 between the GNR and the E&WYUR which stated that the junction which had been constructed at Lofthouse was a temporary one only and that the installation of a permanent one had

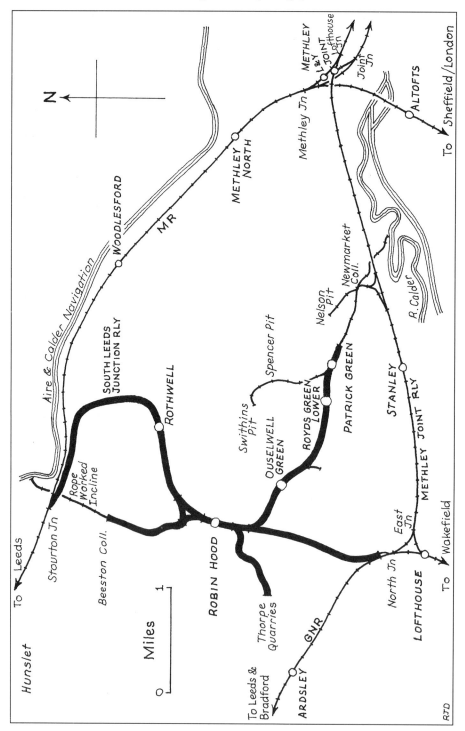

5. The East & West Yorkshire Union Railways – later developments.

been suspended. The GNR wished to build a fly-over junction at that point and had obtained powers in 1889 to do so. It was realised by the GNR that this would be more expensive to build and that Company agreed to bear any additional cost. Needless to say, the fly-over was never built and the 'temporary' junction became permanent.

The E&WYUR obtained another Act in 1894 authorising further abandonments at Ardsley and another reduction in capital, this time to £100,000. The Company's financial position was such that Joseph Charlesworth had to advance money so that the account of Greenwood Teale, the Company's Solicitor, could be settled. The partnership, however, between Teale and Ben Day was dissolved early in 1895, and the Company decided to use the services of the latter, an association which lasted until the end of the Company.

About this time, it was resolved that the Company would work the line themselves after 1 July. Two locomotives were ordered from Manning Wardle of Leeds at a cost of £1,870 each, and two brake-vans from the Birmingham Railway Carriage & Wagon Company at £297 each, all on hire-purchase terms. The locomotives, Manning Wardle works Nos 1307 and 1308 of 1895, became Nos 1 and 2 and were 0-6-0ST engines with 17in x 24in inside cylinders and 4ft diameter driving wheels. They ultimately became LNER Class J84, Nos 3112/3, and were withdrawn in June 1930 and December 1928 respectively.

The South Leeds Junction Railway was opened for mineral traffic on 6 April 1895. A three party Agreement had been reached in January between the two railway companies and Charlesworths that the railways would charge 5d per ton for the carriage of coal from Beeston and Rothwell collieries, and 6d per ton from Robin Hood to the Midland and A&CN at Stourton. The Railway Company would provide the locomotives but not the wagons. This Agreement was signed for the South Leeds Junction Railway by Isaac White as its Chairman. It was arranged, however, that Charlesworths would work the line, until the end of June, in conjunction with that part of the E&WYUR which they were already working.

It was now found necessary to install signalling between Robin Hood and Quarry Sidings and a contract for the new signals was awarded to Saxby

& Farmer and completed within three months, so they cannot have been very extensive. It was also decided to build an engine shed at Rothwell and Whitaker Brothers' tender of £460 was accepted.

Owing to the expansion in traffic, Meyer was ordered to purchase 'a new 14in tank engine' for which Manning Wardle successfully tendered a 15in locomotive. The new locomotive, Manning Wardle works No.1325, was delivered in 1896, becoming No.3. It was an 0-6-0ST with 15in x 22in inside cylinders, and 3ft 6in diameter driving wheels. At first it was reported as satisfactory but it was probably too light and it was sold to Wath Main colliery to become their No.7 in 1899.

At the end of 1895 the Chairman told the share-holders that the Company had been using its own locomotives for the past two months and that the change would be a profitable one. It was decided that the Directors should receive three guineas (£3.15) for each meeting and the Chairman £50 extra per annum.

Negotiations with the GNR Company took place in March with a view to commencing a passenger service to Rothwell, a proposal which had previously been suggested.

The East & West Yorkshire Union Railways (South Leeds Junction Railway Transfer) Act was passed on 2 July 1896 and on that date the SLJR Company was vested in the E&WYUR.

At the end of the year, the shareholders approved a proposal to build a Light Railway, the Newmarket branch, from Robin Hood to Royds Green Lower, where it joined the existing tramway belonging to Charlesworths. The Engineers were again Mammatt & White and the estimated cost was £19,642 15s 2d.

The Public Inquiry into the Light Railway was held before the Light Railway Commissioners at the Grand Hotel, Leeds on 5 February 1897. It was only the second application to be heard since the passing of the new Light Railways Act of 1896. Evidence was given by Joseph Charlesworth, Chairman of the E&WYUR, and by White as Engineer. Meyer said that the E&WYUR was a single line but the earthworks were for a double line. Branches had been opened to Beeston Pit and to Beeston quarries. The extension would form a junction with Charlesworths' tramway and they were prepared to allow traffic to pass. He went on to say that his Directors had authorised him to start a passenger service as soon as Agreements had been made with the main line companies. The GNR was willing to accommodate the traffic but could not do so until Ardsley station had been re-built. It was desirable to have a passenger service on the new branch as soon as passenger traffic started on the main line. He stated that the Company had paid an average dividend of 3¾ per cent. White said that the tramway was now worked by a light locomotive and that his Company had no intention of running heavy trains.

There was practically no opposition and the Commissioners 'had no hesitation in approving the Order'.

Negotiations with the GNR continued for the exchange of passenger traffic at Lofthouse. In June the tender of Whitaker Brothers was provisionally accepted for the construction of the extension and 300 tons of 'slightly defective rails' were bought from Mr Edward Sisterson, another name which appears frequently in this story.

An Agreement was signed in August between the E&WYUR Company and J. & J. Charlesworth that the latter would send all coal from their Newmarket, Nelson and Spencer pits to all places on the GNR and MR over the new line. The E&WYUR agreed to charge not more than 1d per ton above the rate already in force from Robin Hood Colliery. The Railway Company would provide the engines but not the wagons. Traffic to the NER or L&YR, via the Methley Joint Line, was not included.

At the half-yearly meeting, it was stated that the Directors wished to commence passenger trains but there was delay, as agreement had not been reached with the other companies concerned.

Charlesworths now informed the Company that they would be unable to accommodate further traffic at their Rothwell Haigh sidings; the Directors, therefore, decided that it would be necessary to arrange for a direct junction with the Midland.

The Light Railway Order was confirmed by the Board of Trade on 14 December 1897 for a line, nearly two miles long, from Robin Hood to Royds Green Lower. It had to be completed within three years and the Company was allowed to raise a further £26,600, of which £6,600 might be in Debenture stock. This was therefore also the second Light Railway to be authorised after the passing of the Light Railways Act.

In the following February, Rothwell District Council met the Board with a view to promoting the passenger service. It was decided to make a joint approach to the Midland Company to see if some arrangement could be secured for the interchange of passenger traffic with the Midland. A little later, a plan was prepared and approved for a junction with the Midland at Stourton. It was also decided that the Company should try to acquire Charlesworth's tramway from Royds Green to Bottom Boat on the A&CN. By September, no satisfactory reply had been received from the GNR or Midland with regard to the through running of passenger trains. Meyer recommended that powers should be sought to extend to Hunslet to connect with the trams of Leeds Corporation.

With further growth in traffic it was resolved in September 1898 to purchase another locomotive from Manning Wardle at £2,250, 'similar to No.4, recently supplied'. The author has been unable to find any reference in the Minutes to the purchase of No.4 which had occurred earlier in the year. The two engines (Manning Wardle works Nos 1398 and 1433 of 1898 and 1899) numbered 4 and 5, were 0-6-2ST locomotives with 17in x 24in inside cylinders and 3ft 9in diameter driving wheels. No.6 (Manning Wardle works No.1434 of 1899) was ordered almost immediately afterwards. Nos 5 and 6 became LNER Class N19. No.6 was withdrawn on being taken over; No.5 became LNER No.3115 and was withdrawn in 1928.

The Secretary was ordered, at the end of 1899, to obtain estimates for signalling and interlocking in order to obtain the Certificate of the Board of Trade necessary for the working of passenger traffic. These plans were probably turned down, as the Secretary next submitted to the Directors plans prepared by Mr Ellis, of the GNR, for doubling; for signalling; altering the junctions at Lofthouse; and for providing passenger accommodation. It was decided to carry out this work as soon as possible.

Early in 1899 land was acquired for the improvement of the tramway to Charlesworths' Nelson Pit. At the same time, the E&WYUR decided to alter the tramway to the Methley Joint Railway and to the A&CN, which belonged to Charlesworths, to ease its gradient and remove a level crossing over the busy Wakefield–Aberford road,

6. An 'Austerity' class J94 0-6-0ST shunts at Robin Hood. *P. Cookson*

replacing it by a bridge to carry the road over the railway. The Railway Company spent £12,500, including the provision of extra sidings over which it never exercised any legal right. For all this, there was no written agreement, except for the payment of £45 per annum wayleave to Major Calverley for the use of the railway. Joseph Charlesworth was Chairman both of the Railway Company and the Colliery Company.

Plans were submitted at the end of the year, under the Light Railways Act, for the proposed extension to Thwaite Gate. Another locomotive, which became the second No.3, similar to Nos 1 and 2, was ordered from Manning Wardle (works number 1489) at a price of £2,450. This engine never received a LNER number, being withdrawn immediately on being taken over in 1923.

Isaac White, a Director and former Engineer to the Company, died on 23 December 1899, at the early age of 48. Zachariah Yewdall, a partner in the legal firm of Day & Yewdall was elected a Director in his place. D. S. Hartmann was now appointed Engineer, but it is not known how much engineering training or knowledge he possessed.

The Public Inquiry for the Light Railway was held in Wakefield on 5 March 1900. Ben Day was again the Solicitor and Mammatt & White the Engineers. The E&WYUR applied for a line about a mile long from the termination of their railway to Thwaite Gate, Leeds, near to the junction of the Pontefract and Wakefield roads and a short extension from there to Forge Place, Low Road, Hunslet, to serve the works of the Leeds Forge Company. This firm is not to be confused with the Leeds Forge Co. at Armley, Leeds, although there was almost certainly a family connection between the two concerns. It was said in evidence that the only means of conveyance available to the people of Rothwell was by wagonettes which were frequently filled and they were forced to walk. Charles

7. The crossing of the Thorpe branch and the Leeds–Wakefield road (now A61).
About 1905. Note the single-track electric tram line and hoarding with 'J & J Charlesworth Ltd.
Robin Hood Collieries'. *J. Goodchild*

Coghlan, Managing Director of the Leeds Forge Company and one of the promoters of the SLJR, was convinced the lines were necessary; the opposition said it was for the convenience of Leeds Forge and not for the benefit of the public. S. R. Kay, now a partner in the firm of Mammatt, White & Kay, estimated the cost at £26,000 and said that stations would be provided at Stourton and Thwaite Gate and that there was already a platform at Rothwell which could be used for passenger traffic. Powers were also sought to allow the working of the existing railways as Light Railways. The Commissioners were prepared to recommend the granting of the Order, providing clauses were agreed for the protection of interested parties.

This Inquiry was followed immediately afterwards and at the same place by another into a further application from the Brackenhill Light Railway (see Chapter 7).

An interesting item from the 'Journal' of the Company at this time, reads 'Locomotive hire from the Yorkshire District Light Railways Syndicate, £102' – another of Meyer's companies. This was probably *Cawood* which had been made redundant on the taking over of the Cawood, Wistow & Selby Light Railway by the NER.

The shareholders' meeting of February 1901 was told that Joseph Charlesworth was seriously ill and the Chair was taken by Charles E. Charlesworth. He said that the Light Railway Order from the Board of Trade was expected daily but that the Company had had 'cruel opposition from the Great Northern Railway, the Aire & Calder Navigation and others, in their efforts to secure land for the extension'. 'When they reached Hunslet' he said 'they would be able to secure more

8. From the same viewpoint on 20 February 1961. The tramline has gone, but note improvements in road surface and lamp standards (to say nothing of the flagman's dress). The houses are the same. *P. Cookson*

merchandise and their proposed passenger service would then be assured because they could run in conjunction with the Leeds Tramways at Thwaite Gate'. The *Wakefield Herald* reported that in three or four months a service of trains from Wellington (Midland) Station, Leeds, via Robin Hood and Rothwell to Newmarket, near Stanley, would be commenced.

The Secretary was ordered in March to purchase a steam wagon to cart brewery traffic at Rothwell at a price of not more than £400.

Joseph Charlesworth died on 27 May and he was succeeded as Chairman by Charles E. Charlesworth. John Stobart Charlesworth, C. E. Charlesworth's eldest son, joined the Board. Meyer now became Managing Director at a salary of £300 per annum; this represented a fall in income but, as he was becoming increasingly involved in other activities,

he was probably now devoting less time to the E&WYUR, as new full-time officials were employed. Thomas C. Mander was appointed Secretary and Traffic Manager and D. S. Hartmann was now styled Superintendent of the Line.

The Light Railway Order was confirmed in June 1901; the existing railways could now be run as Light Railways, but passenger trains were not to run north of Thwaite Lane. An increase of capital of £9,000 was approved.

Events now moved quickly in another direction. The Midland appeared to find the possibility of competition unwelcome and promptly agreed to discuss the installation of a junction at Stourton and the running of passenger trains to Wellington station at Leeds.

At the second General Meeting of the year the Chairman said that the gradient between Rothwell and Stourton would have to be improved and other works would be needed to satisfy the Board of Trade. A passenger station would also have to be built at Stourton. A shareholder mentioned the rapid expansion of the electric tramway system. The Chairman replied that it had been duly considered and the Directors were satisfied that a considerable passenger traffic would be the result. They would tap a large population at Rothwell and Lofthouse and would earn revenue by carrying numerous workmen to and from their employment. He added that one engine and a couple of cars capable of conveying sixty passengers were the only additions to the rolling stock required. The Directors were authorised to issue £30,000 of 4 per cent Preference stock.

There was a decrease in traffic due to the coal tax and the dividend was reduced to 2½ per cent. The Directors' fees, however, were increased to £500 a year.

Towards the end of the year the *Railway Magazine* wrote that a service of passenger trains running direct from the Wellington Midland Station and through the mining hamlet of Robin Hood and Rothwell to Newmarket, near Stanley, was being arranged and stations at Rothwell and Robin Hood and near Stanley were being built. 'We congratulate Mr Meyer on the new enterprise'.

Early in 1902, the steam wagon was sent to the works for general repair. The sum of £84 9s 6d was received from the Isle of Axholme Light Railway for the supply of ashes – another Meyer transaction?

The Chairman, at the Autumn meeting, stated optimistically that it was intended to provide 'comfortable' passenger carriages and the service was expected to be ready next January or February. There would be stations at Rothwell and Thwaite Gate and, with a stop at Hunslet, they would run into the Midland Station in Leeds. He continued that on Saturdays some 2,000 persons came into Leeds and, more cautiously, that doubtless it would be a large item entailing at the outset some difficulty.

It was resolved in May 1903 that passenger traffic on the 'South Leeds Railway' be pressed forward with greater urgency and that it should certainly be open for August Bank Holiday.

The new junction at Stourton was opened for goods traffic on 1 November and passed for

passenger traffic on 1 December. This, of course, rendered the construction of the proposed branch to Hunslet superfluous and no more is heard of it. It was resolved to open 'forthwith' the Newmarket branch for passenger traffic. 'Ordinary accommodation' would be provided at Ouzelwell Green but only a platform at Patrick Green. This is the first mention of these places. Ouzelwell Green will be referred to many times later and Patrick Green appears to have been another name for Royds Green Lower. At the end of the year a tender for the signalling of the Newmarket branch was submitted.

The Board decided to purchase from A. M. Terry of Newcastle, for £410, a secondhand Black, Hawthorn 0-4-0ST locomotive, stated in the Minutes to have been built in 1879. This was, in fact, Black, Hawthorn works No.424 of 1877, supplied new to William Doxford & Sons, Pallion Shipyard, Sunderland. It had 12in x 19in outside cylinders and driving wheels of 3ft 2in diameter.

The year 1904 was a traumatic one for the Company. It opened happily on New Year's Day with the receipt of the report from Major Pringle, the Railway Inspecting Officer, allowing passenger traffic on the railway. It was decided to commence the service on Monday 4 January, with four trains a day including Sundays. The official opening was followed by a luncheon in the waiting room of Rothwell Station for the Directors and invited guests. The trains were powered by Midland 0-4-4T engines Nos 6 (re-numbered to 1226 in 1907) and 1265 (1239) with coaches hired from the Midland. At this time the office of the Company was moved to Rothwell Station.

Early in the year E&WYUR locomotive No.1, was overhauled by Manning Wardle 'for the new service of passenger trains'. A vacuum brake was fitted and the valve gear was altered to Marshall's – a modified Joy gear.

Hartmann resigned in February 'owing to ill-health'. The illness must have been short-lived or his resignation was not accepted, as, by the end of March, he was ordered 'to prepare plans to restore land'.

The Black, Hawthorn engine was reported in March to be 'in very bad condition and was to be taken out of steam'. Estimates were to be obtained for its repair. In May the Minutes state: 'no more money to be spent on Black, Hawthorn loco-

9. Rothwell station on 31 January 1932 looking towards Stourton. *Collection A. L. Barnett*

motive, until further orders'. In July it was decided to have locomotive No.3 fitted with the vacuum brake, 'to relieve No.1 when necessary'. It is doubtful if this was carried out.

The Sunday passenger service was withdrawn from 4 September. The Company was now losing £200 a month on the passenger service. The trains were being used by only a dozen or so passengers. The Directors, therefore, decided that it should cease after 30 September. It is generally stated that the failure was due to competition from the electric trams, but the Wakefield to Thwaite Gate service did not commence until late August and the through service into Leeds started only in June 1905. At the same time, there was a heavy decrease in mineral traffic.

In September 'two coaching carriages of the Company' were to be sold for £100 each, and in October the Black, Hawthorn locomotive was ordered 'to be sold for what she will fetch'. It eventually came into the hands of Sir Robert McAlpine & Sons.

At the end of that month Meyer resigned as Managing Director but he retained his seat on the Board. He probably felt responsible for the disastrous venture into passenger carriage but, as will be seen from what has been written, the Directors had been proposing this almost from the inception of the railway. Mander also resigned as Secretary.

The records of the Company are tantalisingly incomplete in many details. It is the author's opinion, without direct evidence, that the passenger trains to Leeds were worked by Midland stock and that at, or about the same time, there was a workmen's service on the Newmarket branch worked by E&WYUR's locomotives and carriages.

Early in January 1905 the Company decided to retain working at Stourton sidings and it was reported that a tank engine of Charlesworths, undergoing repair at Manning Wardles, might be suitable for purchase at a price of £300, plus the cost of repair.

W. H. Wilson was appointed Secretary in place of T. C. Mander.

Later in the month the Board of Trade granted permission to the Company to run the line on the old system as a mineral railway. At the same time, Meyer was asked to treat with the Railway Signal Company to see if they would purchase all the surplus signalling. Further tidying up took place, as it was resolved to sell the wooden station at Stourton and 'anything that can be spared' from Patrick Green.

It was now decided to buy J. & J. Charlesworth's locomotive, *The Brother*, at a price of £1,000 payable by three installments of £334. This was an 0-6-0ST, built by Hudswell, Clarke, works number 362 of 1889. The Agreement to purchase was sealed a week later on 1 February but, nevertheless, the deal must have fallen through as the locomotive was hired from Charlesworths for a short period in July. Locomotive No.1, after it had been fitted with Marshall's valve gear, was able to haul five or six more wagons than the other engines (it was later reported to be hauling 25 per cent more than the others). It was, therefore, decided to convert No.5 in the same way; it is doubtful if this was carried out. There can, however, be no doubt that the gear was successful, at any rate at first, but it appears to have been removed some time later as there is no mention of it in *Locomotives of the L.N.E.R.* Mr Terry now reported to the Board on the condition of the Black, Hawthorn locomotive at the time when he sold it to the Company. He thought he could help in its disposal for about £270.

In August 1905, C. E. Charlesworth announced his resignation from the Board after fourteen years of service. The *Wakefield Herald* forecast that, as his firm supplied the bulk of the traffic on the railway, his son, J. S. Charlesworth would succeed him in the Chair. Their guess was wrong; that position, which he retained until the end of the Company, went to Z. Yewdall.

At the end of the year tenders were invited from various firms for the supply of a new four-wheel engine for use on the Newmarket Extension Railway, that is, from Patrick Green to Nelson Pit. About the same time, a Hudswell, Clarke 0-6-0ST locomotive named *Success* was hired from Charlesworths; its works number was 341 of 1890.

Approaches were made to Messrs Charlesworth for the purchase of the railway from Patrick Green to Newmarket Pit. The price asked, however, was 'too onerous for the Company' and it was resolved to seek Compulsory Powers from the Light Railway Commissioners.

Edward Sisterson was invited to join the Board in February 1906. The following month the resignation of J. S. Charlesworth 'was accepted with regret'. This marks the end of the long association between the Charlesworth family and the E&WYUR Company and possibly an indication of a certain amount of friction between the two companies. Ben Day became a Director in his place; Sisterson was made Vice-Chairman.

Manning Wardle agreed to the cancellation of an order for a small locomotive in April. The Black, Hawthorn engine was to be repaired and sold for £250. A motor dray was to be bought from Bentleys of Woodlesford for £300 but, two months later, the purchase of a new 'motor dray' from Messrs Mann's Patent Steam Cart and Wagon Company of Leeds was authorised at a price of £350. Although described as a 'motor dray', it was almost certainly a steam wagon. The deal was to be financed by the Yorkshire Railway Wagon Company. It is not clear if this indicates one or two purchases.

Further hiring of engines took place, both from Charlesworths and from the Midland. Armitage Brothers were paid £1 for assisting at an accident at Thorpe.

A Wharncliffe Meeting (that is a statutory meeting of shareholders to approve proposals before they could be considered in a Parliamentary Bill or a Light Railway Order) took place on 21 November 1906. The purpose of the proposed Light Railway Order was to obtain powers to take over certain existing railways belonging to Messrs Charlesworth and to legalise others belonging to the Company but built without authority. At this meeting Mr A. Herbert, who later became a Director, said he represented two-thirds of the holders of the 4 per cent Preference shares which included such well-known concerns as the Scottish Widows' Life Assurance Co, the Sun Life Insurance Co, and the trustees of the Railway Clearing House Superannuation Fund (four per cent was considered a good return at that time). He stated that 'the branches were made without any authority from Parliament, without any authority from the Light Railway Commissioners and, so far as I can gather, without even asking the share-holders. But it was not denied that the branches were profitable.'

The estimated cost of acquiring Charlesworth's railways etc. was £34,181 10s and it was desirable to raise a further £30,000. Herbert was worried that this increase in capital would prejudice the Preference shareholders.

J. and W. H. Charlesworth voted against the resolution but later withdrew their opposition so that the vote appeared unanimous. The plans were signed by 'D. S. Hartmann, Engineer'. He was paid £22 16s 9d for preparing the plans and sections.

William Hargreaves died in January and Abraham Armitage, one of the partners in the quarries and brickworks at Thorpe, took his place on the Board.

The Public Inquiry, before the Light Railway Commissioners, was heard in Leeds on 30 January 1907. The E&WYUR sought powers to take over and re-align the existing mineral railway from Royds Green Lower (Patrick Green) to its junction with the Methley Joint line, to take over the branch to Swithen's Colliery, already used by the E&WYUR, to take over the Thorpe branch (opened 1890), and the Beeston branch railway. Counsel for the E&WYUR said that the earlier tramways were primitive, ill-adapted and quite inadequate for working. The E&WYUR had spent £12,500 on improving lines which did not belong to them. The land belonged to Major Calverley and was on lease with eighteen years to run, the Railway company would have to expend a large amount of money which would eventually go to Major Calverley but it was only right that the Railway Company should benefit itself. The collieries (Swithen's and Newmarket Haigh Moor Pits) now belonged to Messrs Briggs but Charlesworths were in a position to block the traffic. The line was worked by an inadequate system of signalling and it was proposed to install electric signalling. The Company wished to acquire land on the Aire & Calder Navigation and

10. An Ardsley–Stourton mineral train headed by ex-GNR class J6 0-6-0 No.64170 near Rothwell in February 1961. *P. Cookson*

build a shipping staith there but Major Calverley had control of the traffic which was not in the public interest.

Yewdall, in evidence, said that there were frequent delays due to the dual control. The E&WYUR could not take further traffic because of the conditions of the lease.

Meyer said the line was single and could not be worked safely for the men unless the working was in one hand. For many years they had been excluded from carrying public traffic. There were large brickworks at Thorpe, and Rothwell was now an important place.

The Chairman of the Commissioners stated that they appreciated the difficulties of the promoters but he regretted that they had not shown an overwhelming case on behalf of the public. He hoped that arrangements could be made to work the railway as one line. The application was refused.

Powers for the raising of further money were, however, allowed and this went forward to the Board of Trade in July. The Light Railway Order, confirmed on 4 November 1907, authorised the Company to raise an additional £14,000 on mortgage.

In June 1907, it was decided to sell the passenger coaches (the same two?). Next came a proposal from Messrs Charlesworth to take over the working of the line; the Board said it had no powers to agree to this, even if it were desirable.

In October the Directors, not discouraged, decided to try to get powers to build a new line of their own to the Methley Joint Railway. They would apply for an Order, with Messrs Briggs' support, to construct a line, over which Briggs would have Running Powers, from Royds Green Lower to the Joint Line and give Briggs access to water. Briggs did not object to the E&WYUR taking over their line.

It was minuted on 25 September 1908 that the Swithen's branch had been sold to Messrs Briggs for £1,500 (probably by Charlesworths).

In the following year Oleine Ltd, one of Sebastian Meyer's companies of which more will be heard later, applied for a siding at Ouzelwell Green on the Newmarket branch. The Railway Company agreed to this at a cost of not more than £290, provided Oleine completed the purchase of

the site for their factory from the Railway Company at a price of £360.

Plans were produced by Hartmann, now Superintendent and Resident Engineer, at the end of 1910 for a line, just over a mile long, from Royds Green Lower to the Methley Joint line, at an estimated cost of £11,139 10s. The Public Inquiry was held in Leeds on 19 July 1911. It was again stated by Counsel, that the Light Railway Order of 1897 was not carried further because it joined the tramway, the property of Charlesworths, and the E&WYUR had made an Agreement with Charlesworths to carry the colliery traffic, using the tramway. This had been found unsatisfactory and the Railway Company had now spent £14,000 in improving the line. The Company had spent money on land on which they had not even a lease, not even an Agreement. They paid rent but had nothing in writing. The explanation was that, while the Charlesworths were directors and principal shareholders, it was thought that everything would work smoothly. It was now admitted that there was congestion and that trucks on the running line might take an hour to clear; at times it was almost impossible to get traffic through. The Commissioners, in 1907, had suggested that negotiations should take place to improve working but this had come to nothing. The Agreement with Major Calverley prevented ordinary traffic being put on the line but the new Oleine factory wished to put a considerable amount onto the line. As the Company had failed in its application to acquire the tramway, it now proposed to build an additional through, independent line.

Meyer stated that they picked up the old tramway at Royds Green Lower and that they had tried to work it on the old system for a few months but it really was impossible. The metals were too light and the gradients too heavy. They had altered the gradients from 1 in 26 to 1 in 45, abolished one level crossing and re-constructed the line in a much more substantial way. They, the E&WYUR, paid rent but had no tenure of the land. They now proposed to have a line of their own and not take away the rights of the Charlesworths.

Charlesworths again said that all that was needed was additional siding accommodation and that the proposed line would prevent them providing this. It would also block off access to

11. A railtour at Rothwell, on 21 September 1958, headed by Class J6 0-6-0s nos 64222 and 64268.
J. F. Henton

their pumping station. As had been stated, Charlesworths had sold their Newmarket Haigh Moor Pits to Briggs; an Agreement, at the insistence of Major Calverley, was made in 1906 that Briggs might make lines of their own from the collieries down to the Methley Joint line and to the river. Charlesworths said, probably not openly, that 'it is one thing to have interference from a private line and quite another from a public railway company'.

This view was taken by the Commissioners who stated that they understood that Charlesworths 'really *bona fide*' intended to remedy the congestion and provide sufficient outlet for the E&WYUR. On that understanding, they rejected the application. There is evidence that additional sidings were provided a few years later.

At the end of the year Hartmann was again asked to produce plans for a new route to the Methley Joint line but this proposal appears to have been allowed to die a natural death.

A. Herbert was elected a Director in 1913 to represent the London shareholders.

An interesting event took place in 1914. The colliers of Rothwell Haigh Colliery decided to run a holiday excursion. Permission from the Board of Trade had to be obtained and Major Pringle issued a favourable report. The GNR required an indemnity from the E&WYUR. That Company asked for a fare of not less than 4d per passenger. The excursion duly took place on 4 July and, in the end, the GNR paid 6d per passenger. Unfortunately, the author has been unable to find the destination of the train but, as the GNR was involved, it was probably Skegness.

Later, locomotive No.6 was hired to Samuelson's Littletown Colliery, County Durham.

In 1916 Oleine Ltd purchased a further acre of land from the E&WYUR for £365 and the Railway Company agreed to construct a siding. The Agreement was signed for Oleine Ltd by Philip J. Meyer and D. S. Hartmann.

Locomotive No.4 was extensively re-built by Manning, Wardle in 1919. It was converted into a 0-6-0ST, eventually becoming LNER Class J85,

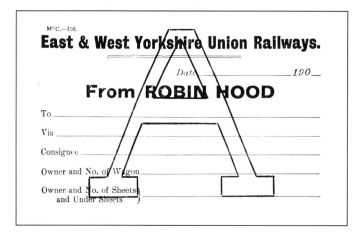

Mᶜᶜ.—110.

East & West Yorkshire Union Railways.

Date_____190__

From ROBIN HOOD

To_____

Via_____

Consignee_____

Owner and No. of Wagon

Owner and No. of Sheets
and Under Sheets

12. A wagon label for wagons despatched from Robin Hood goods depot. *Collection A. Wilson*

No.3114, and was withdrawn in 1933.

The railway came under Government control during World War I and, at the end of hostilities, received £13,415 compensation.

The last meeting of the Board took place on 21 June 1923. Z. Yewdall took the Chair, and A. Armitage, Ben Day, A. Herbert and S. W. Meyer were present. The Company had paid no dividends from 1903 to 1909, then it paid one per cent, up to two per cent in 1921. The shareholders received, for each £100 of E&WYUR stock held, for 3¾ per cent Debentures, £93 15s of LNER 4 per cent First Guaranteed stock; for 4½ per cent Debentures, £106 5s of LNER 4 per cent First Guaranteed; for 5 per cent Debentures, £125 in the above stock; for 4 per cent E&WYUR Preference shares, £50 in LNER Second Preference and £40 in Preference Ordinary and £75 in Deferred Ordinary. The Company was amalgamated into the LNER on 1 July 1923.

By 1925 Oleine Ltd were unfortunately in financial difficulties and the LNER decided that it was necessary to determine Agreements entered into by the E&WYUR in 1910 and 1916 with that Company. Formal notice was sent by the LNER to the Liquidator, L. D. Kidson, that the Agreements would be terminated as from 26 April 1926.

The Newmarket branch was closed on 9 December 1963. The line from Robin Hood to Stourton closed 'to all intents and purposes' from June 1961 owing to engineering works on the abortive Stourton marshalling yard; it did not close officially until October 1966. The remainder of the E&WYUR was closed on 3 October 1966.

As both the E&WYUR and the SLJR were built under ordinary Parliamentary procedure and not as Light Railways, they contained many engineering features. The main line of the E&WYUR was constructed as a single line but the earthworks, etc. were constructed for double track and it was quickly doubled as traffic developed. Both Railways ran through a fairly densely populated, industrial area, so bridges were frequent and were generally overline ones. The course of the SLJR was almost a semi-circle, part of it in cutting and part of it steeply graded (with the load) at 1 in 67. There was a speed limit of 15 miles per hour over the whole system.

The branches were built under Light Railway Orders, or under no authority at all, and these were all single lines. The Newmarket branch was worked by Staff and Ticket between Robin Hood and Patrick Green. There was a passing place at Patrick Green and, from there to Newmarket Colliery, the line was worked by one engine in steam. The branch was steeply graded, the ruling gradient being 1 in 44 'against the load' towards Robin Hood, (although it is probable that coal was carried in both directions). Only 12 or 14 loaded wagons could be brought up to Patrick Green at one time, necessitating a further trip if the load was greater. There was a level crossing at Patrick Green which required the use of a flagman and there were several occupation crossings. An overline bridge carried the busy Wakefield–Aberford road over the railway, replacing the former level-crossing of the old colliery tramway.

The other branches were worked under 'No Block' regulations. They were severely graded and curved and as they 'are also used by private engines, when necessary, drivers must keep a sharp look-out and be prepared to stop at any time'. The Thorpe branch crossed the very busy Wakefield–Leeds road (with its electric trams) by a level-crossing, also protected by a flagman. A crossing over Milner

Lane was unprotected. The class N19 0-6-2Ts were the favourite engines on the branch, on account of their shorter wheelbase. Another branch ran from a triangle, north of Robin Hood, to Beeston Colliery.

Returning to the main line, there were sidings at Lofthouse, and an extensive layout at Robin Hood. This was followed by the triangle already mentioned and, at the base of this, there was a three-road engine shed which closed in July 1926. There were further sidings at Stourton and, on the branch, at Patrick Green.

Robin Hood was the centre of the system and Rothwell was the administrative headquarters.

13. Sebastian Meyer aged about 50.
A photograph taken about 1906 when he was Sheriff of York.
Collection G. Sellers

CHAPTER THREE

Family Interlude

WHEN Meyer left the Hull & Barnsley Railway in 1884 to become Secretary of the East & West Yorkshire Union Railways Company he took up residence in Leeds and thus began an association with that City which was second only to that with his adopted City of York. It is probable that even at that early date, he was touring the countryside with a view to opening it up by Light Railways. It is a fact, however, that he met Grace Hutchinson, the daughter of William and Lucy Hutchinson of Gunby, near Selby. William Hutchinson was a prosperous farmer, County Councillor and Justice of the Peace; the family were of old yeoman Quaker stock. He married Grace at Bubwith on 3 June 1886. He was thirty years of age and she twenty-five. The witnesses were Henry J. Meyer, a younger brother from London and John Burtt of York. Burtt was a distant relative of Mrs Hutchinson. Philip Burtt (the exact relationship has not been traced) later became a close friend and neighbour of Meyer and a partner in the milk factory in Northallerton. He too was a Quaker and rose to be Assistant Manager of the North Eastern Railway.

A year later Philip John Meyer was born in Bramley, Leeds and, in the following year, Sebastian Burtt Meyer was born in South Milford. The family moved to York in 1893 and during 1894 it was completed by a daughter, Ellen Grace.

Meyer himself was brought up in the Lutheran tradition. Whilst living in Hull he would have had no difficulty in finding a church of that denomination. Afterwards he attended the Church of England but, quite without prejudice, he acted as organist in a Wesleyan Chapel. In 1899, at the age of forty-three, he decided that he and his children

14. 'Brackenhill', Meyer's house in York which he built in 1902. Note the artificial 'bracken hill'. *Author*

should become members of the Society of Friends (Quakers). He told senior representatives of the York Monthly Meeting that he believed that some of his ancestors had suffered for their faith but this may have been a little bit of historical licence. He also told them that, much as he loved music, he had come to believe that its value in religious services was doubtful. His application was approved and he steadily rose to a position of great eminence and respect at the York Monthly Meeting.

Now in a prosperous and assured position, in 1902 he built himself a large family house in St. George's Place, York (with an excellent view of the NER main line) and he lived there until about 1920. The house was named 'Brackenhill' and there is a man-made bracken hill in the garden to this day. It is tempting to suggest that the house was built by money from the Brackenhill Light Railway but that concern showed no financial return until a later period. Meyer must have thought the name attractive. On the other hand he would have received a substantial remuneration for his work in obtaining its Light Railway Order.

The house became an old persons' home run by York City Council but, unfortunately, no trace of the Meyer occupancy remains, apart from the garden and the name. Sadly it was closed on 30 June 1989.

His children were educated at the well-known Quaker school at Ackworth. Philip John Meyer attended the University of Manchester and obtained a B.SC. in Chemistry in 1908 and his younger brother studied at Reading University College and the University of Edinburgh. Philip became the Manager of Oleine Ltd but resigned during World War I to join the Friends' War Victims Relief Committee. He saw ambulance

15. P. R. Meyer's name on a North Lindsey Light Railway notice still extant at West Halton on 20 June 1954. *T. J. Edgington*

service in Italy and in 1918 went to Paris. There he contracted influenzal broncho-pneumonia. As was so common in that dreadful epidemic, he died, like so many other young men and women, within a few hours. His parents did not know of his illness until they heard of his death. They never recovered from the shock.

16. Sebastian Meyer's signature on a share certificate of the E&WYUR with the initials of D. S. Hartmann. The original is in the author's collection. *T. J. Lodge*

17. Meyer in old age, in 1938 aged 82, but still an active musician.
Collection G. Sellers

18. Seahouses station in 1950. *H. P. White*

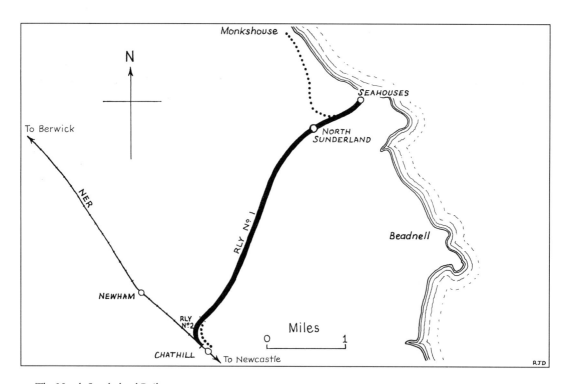

19. The North Sunderland Railway

CHAPTER FOUR

The North Sunderland Railway

THE second railway with which Sebastian Meyer was connected was the North Sunderland Railway. This was first suggested in 1891 when a deputation representing local interests approached the Directors of the North Eastern Railway Company to see if they would build a branch from their main line at Chathill to North Sunderland and the little port of Seahouses for the carriage of fish from the recently constructed harbour at the latter place. It was also hoped that holiday traffic would develop. The deputation was unsuccessful.

On 27 June of the following year, some of the gentry and clergy of the district obtained an Act of Parliament to construct a line about four miles in length to Seahouses from the east side of Chathill station, where there was to be a connection 660 yards long to the NER. The authorised capital was £21,000 in £10 shares with borrowing powers of £7,000 and the first Directors were the Rev. Dixon Dixon-Brown, George Dixon, A. Clark, Robert Simmonds, and James Ewing. The Secretary and Manager was Richard Smith, of Newcastle, and R. Elliott Cooper was Engineer. A prospectus was issued in 1893.

The Minutes of the Directors' meeting of 9 October 1896 reported that there had been correspondence between Meyer and the Secretary of the Company. Unfortunately it is not recorded who

initiated this but it was probably Meyer. Meyer himself had been invited to attend the meeting. Thus began an association which lasted until 1941, the longest between Meyer and any railway in which he was interested. It was noted that Messrs Whitakers, engineers of Leeds, had been over the ground and that they would submit a contract for the construction of the line. Meyer stated, 'I am prepared to obtain a contract (from Whitakers) for the construction of the whole of the Railway for sums not exceeding £19,000, the contractors to be paid in cash and in Lloyds Bonds on the Company.'* This was agreed and Whitakers duly built the line. Later in the month he submitted a contract with Mr Edward Sisterson for permanent way material. Sisterson, who has already been mentioned in chapter 2, was an iron and steel merchant of Newcastle upon Tyne and the goods he supplied were, almost certainly, second-hand. This, too, was the start of another long association between Meyer, Sisterson and the various railway companies in which they became jointly concerned.

Even before the opening of the line, the Directors had ambition for extension. Lord Crewe's Trustees, who had built the harbour at Seahouses, now proposed to lay out a new seaside resort at Monks House about halfway between Seahouses and Bamburgh, to be called St Aidan's-by-the-Sea. In 1897 there was much correspondence between the Board and Meyer and he attended Directors' meetings to discuss an application to the Light Railway Commissioners for a Light Railway to Monks House and the purchase of land there.

The Light Railway Order, which authorised the

* Lloyds Bonds were a means used, chiefly by railway companies, to borrow money or pay their creditors in excess of their authorised capital. The bonds were saleable and the interest was guaranteed to the purchaser but not to the original holder as, strictly speaking, his contract was illegal. They had nothing to do with Lloyds Bank.

20. Chathill station looking south in 1950. North Sunderland train in bay platform headed by ex-NER class Y7 0-4-0T No.68089 on hire from British Railways. *H. P. White*

construction of a railway, about 1½ miles long, from Seahouses to Monks House, was approved on 13 August 1898. It allowed the NSR to be worked as a Light Railway and permitted the raising of a further £10,000 in shares and £3,300 in Debentures. This year, 1898, was an eventful one for the Company; the line was opened for goods traffic on 1 August and for passengers on 14 December. Earlier, the NER had sent an account for £1,950 for work done at Chathill station. Meyer reported that he had been able to get this reduced to £1,000, the first of many similar negotiations with the larger company.

The Company started operations with a Manning Wardle 0-6-0 saddle tank locomotive, works No.1394 of 1898, which they named *Bamburgh*. For many years this engine was the only motive power and when it was out of commission the company had to hire from the NER or its successors. The locomotive was rebuilt by its

makers in 1920. It had a reasonably long life, not being finally scrapped until 1949 by the Motherwell Machinery & Scrap Co. Ltd.

The first passenger rolling stock was five four-wheeled coaches purchased from the Highland Railway but these were not so long-lived as the engine, lasting only until 1911–13. They were replaced by two NER four-wheeled carriages. A further NER coach was purchased in 1924 which later became No.3. The final purchase of passenger stock was three ex-GER carriages in 1937. One of these was withdrawn in 1939, the other two were numbered 1 and 2. Nos 1 and 3 were used on the last train, No.2 being reported 'in a very bad state of repair'. The last remaining three coaches were sold to the South Shields, Marsden & Whitburn Colliery Railway in 1951, where they had a short life as miners' trains ran for only a further two years.

There were few engineering features on the line, the largest being a lightly constructed girder bridge over the Long Nanny burn. There were overline bridges near Fleetham and near Pasturehill carrying unclassified roads and a level crossing to the north of North Sunderland station. According to the deposited plans, the steepest gradients were 1 in 132 and 1 in 150, descending towards Seahouses, but Wright says that the steepest was at 1 in 80, perhaps an example of Meyer's economy. The line was single, worked by 'one engine in steam' and controlled by Staff and Annett's Key. There were no signals except a fixed distant signal approaching Chathill.

The station buildings at North Sunderland and Seahouses were constructed from corrugated iron and the platforms were originally wooden. A small engine shed was built at Seahouses. The Company hoped to provide a small steamer service to the Farne Islands. The year 1898–9 was a busy and successful one for the Company and it made a profit of £46 11s 11½d which was carried forward, an event which was seldom repeated. It was decided to proceed with the extension to Monks House but, in spite of that, nothing was ever done. In July 1899 Meyer 'promised to endeavour to dispose of the Preference Stock within two years;' there was nearly £10,000 of this. Edward Sisterson, who has already been mentioned, was appointed a Director in August 1901 and eight years later he was elected Chairman in place of Colonel C. Rowlandson, a position he retained until 1919.

With the turn of the century the railway settled down to a more or less uneventful and somewhat impecunious existence for several years before finally falling into debt.

In 1912 Meyer and Colonel S. M. Rowlandson, son of the late Colonel C. Rowlandson, were invited to join the Board; Meyer remained a Director until 1941.

The railway came under Government control in 1914 and, at the end of hostilities, received £1,267 in compensation for arrears of maintenance,

etc during the period of Government use. In October 1921 Meyer reported to the Board that he had attended a dozen meetings of the Association of Smaller Railway Companies in London and, representing two other companies besides the North Sunderland, he proposed to charge one-third of his expenses; this was agreed to.

This Association had been formed in 1919 to ensure that the estimated receipts of smaller owning companies were not reduced prior to amalgamation with larger companies and also to see that they received a fair proportion of compensation under the 1921 Railways Act. The Association was a motley collection of minor railway companies. Meyer's other two concerns were the East & West Yorkshire Union and the North Lindsey Light; the Dearne Valley was not represented. Colonel H. F. Stephens' only contribution to the Association was on behalf of the Festiniog Railway which also had been under Government control. As all matters of compensation had been settled by 1923, the Association could only have had a short life.

The North Sunderland Railway escaped the Grouping net, no doubt because it was a Light Railway without connections with any main line company.

Bradshaw's Railway Shareholders' Manual for 1923, its last year of publication, reported, as it had done many times before, that the NSR had not yet paid any dividends on its Ordinary or Preferred shares. Richard Smith, who had been Secretary and Manager of the Company since its inception in 1893, died on 10 February 1933 at the age of 80. His son, Fred W. Smith, was appointed Secretary and Accountant in his place at a salary of £70 per annum plus £15 for office accommodation. This year was a momentous one for the Company in many ways. In the previous year Messrs Armstrong Whitworth had built a prototype diesel-electric shunting engine, works number D10. It was a 15-ton, 100-horsepower machine powered by an

Miles	Down.	Week Days only.					Miles	Up.	Week Days only.				
		gov|mrn|aft	Sats.	aft|aft|aft|			gov|mrn|aft	Sats.	aft|aft|aft
¾	Chathill ......dep.	8 20|10 15|1 30|	3 45|5 15|6 55|....|....	4	Seahouses........dep.	7 40|9 35|1 0|	2 47|4 30|5 45|....
4	Seahouses ....arr.	8 35|10 30|1 45|	4 0|5 30|7 10|....|....	4	Chathill 732, 733 arr.	7 52|9 50|1 15|	3 2|4 45|6 0|....

21. North Sunderland timetable, from May 1914 'Bradshaw'.

Armstrong-Saurer engine. After initial trials it was lent to the NSR for further testing. It was later returned to the Scotswood Works and was scrapped in 1954. The design was successful and Armstrong's built several more, some with slight modification and one was purchased by the NSR, as will be described. Fortunately, two of the type have been preserved.

Possibly as a form of 'stock-taking' after Richard Smith's death, Meyer submitted a report to his fellow directors which they accepted. It was dated 16 November 1933, from College Road, Ripon, where he now resided; it should be noted that he was 77 years of age at that time. He said that the rails and joints were good but the sleepers poor and he recommended that second-hand ones should be bought from the LNER. The ballast and side ditches required considerable work. There were no signals on the line, except at Chathill. There were facing points for which an Annett's Key had been provided at considerable cost. He continued:

It (the Annett's Key system) has been abandoned by our men for many years and is now in a very bad state. It is absolutely necessary and ought not to have been discarded. (This was later restored.) When the line was constructed, a run-round road was provided 28 chains from Chathill. Many years ago this system was abandoned, the run-round road was scrapped and a system of working substituted which involved using the LNER shunting neck on a rising gradient and letting the engine get at the head of the train by means of fly shunting. I have been unable to discover on whose authority the change was made but, in my opinion, it has many disadvantages compared with the system originally sanctioned. In foggy or slippery weather, it seems dangerous. It involves the LNER signals and the NSR providing three men when two would do, as the fly shunting can only be done by having one man on the locomotive, another with a shunting pole to uncouple the moving coaches at the right moment and a third man to manipulate the point levers and throw the moving wagons and coaches into different sidings. It is the kind of operation you may risk if you have no alternative.

In my judgment, it is unnecessary to have two men on the footplate. In my opinion, the fireman should be dispensed with. The run-round method of working should be reverted to and instructions have been given to the platelayers to start at once restoring this road.

I propose to take charge of the engineering and operating side of the line.

The Board gave him the title of Managing Director, with a salary of £200 per annum and an extra £60 for travelling and hotel expenses, with effect from 28 October 1933. His first action in that capacity was to order from Armstrong Whitworth a 'diesel oil electric 15 ton shunting locomotive' at the end of the year. The total price was £1,914 16s, £1,000 down, with three further payments in six, twelve and eighteen months of £317 12s, £311 12s and £285 12s, respectively. These included hire-purchase interest at four per cent. The locomotive, Armstrong Whitworth's works number D35 of 1933, was named *Lady Armstrong* after the wife of the Chairman. It was claimed to be the first diesel-electric passenger locomotive in the country. *Bamburgh* was put on reserve. At first the diesel appeared successful but it soon proved to be a not unmixed blessing. There are stories of conscientious staff working long hours of overtime to have it in working order for the following morning and there were frequent visits to its home works at Newcastle or to the LNER Darlington shops. At first, *Bamburgh* was put into steam again as a replacement.

The finances of the Company did not improve and in 1936 Meyer agreed to relinquish payment for his 'expert services'. In place of this he agreed to take over the coal business of Mr Cuthbertson at Seahouses, which was estimated to bring in about £160 a year. In July Meyer reported that Mr F. W. Smith's term of office as Secretary had expired on 30 June and that he, Meyer, had taken over the Secretary's and Accountant's work. £2,763 4s 4d was now overdue to the LNER.

Early in 1937 Godfrey S. Duffield of Durham was appointed Secretary in an honorary capacity, his expenses only to be paid. By the end of 1938 the arrears due to the LNER were £4,600, and it was agreed that independent accountants should report on the position.

Matters came to a head about the middle of 1939 when Mr C. N. Jenkin Jones, General Manager of the North Eastern Area of the LNER, issued a five-point ultimatum:

1. Meyer was to cease as Manager from the end of July.
2. On the termination of his contract, which was in force for five years from 30 April 1936, the proceeds of the coal business should become part of the revenue of the Light Railway.
3. The LNER would nominate one of its officers as

22. The same train as in fig 20 viewed from the other end. The nearest coach is the five-compartment ex-NER composite. *H. P. White*

Manager of the Company.

4. The NSR would pay £10 per annum in respect of management.

5. The Directors' fees would be waived but Meyer would receive £15 a year.

The terms had to be accepted and H. F. Sanderson, District Goods Manager at Newcastle, took over as Manager. (Sanderson later acted in a similar capacity on the Easingwold Railway.) Meyer's fellow Directors, Lord Armstrong and Captain de Burgh, added the following note to the appropriate minute, which encomium is worthy of reproduction in full:

Mr Sebastian William Meyer joined the Board on 29 October 1912 having before then and since 1896, acted professionally for the Company in settling the contract for the works, supervising construction, purchasing rolling stock and land, and securing Capital. About £16,000 was introduced by him for land and railway.

Since the death of the late Mr R. Smith in 1933, Mr Meyer has managed the railway to the entire satisfaction of his colleagues. He has obtained considerable advances in the traffic allowance from the LNER in addition to allowance of about £1,600 in respect of previous traffic undersettlements with that Company. He has reorganised the Railway which, in

1933, was in a very bad state of repair for want of funds and he has considerably reduced the margin between revenue and expenditure. He assents to the above proposals as he hopes that the further economies indicated may be sufficient to enable the Company to survive.

He was then paid £15 Director's fees for the year, plus £35 expenses up to 31 July 1939, when he retired from management, but he remained a Director. However, the last recorded meeting of the Directors took place soon afterwards on 16 November 1939. By this time the country was involved in the Second World War. Strangely, traffic, at least goods traffic, increased on the NSR although passenger revenue was greatly reduced.

A meeting between Mr Meyer and Mr Sanderson, in his capacity as Manager, took place on 27 July 1942 at Carnforth where Meyer was now residing. He informed Sanderson that he had sold all his shares in the railway and was no longer a Director. Certain documents had not been obtained and Meyer was requested to arrange for them to be handed over. This appears to be the end of Meyer's connection with the NSR which had lasted 46 years. It was also the end of his railway

23. The North Sunderland's diesel locomotive Lady Armstrong delivered by
Armstrong Whitworth in 1933. *Collection G. Sellers*

24. Ex-NER four-wheel coach. Note it is classified as second class.
Collection H. C. Casserley.

career, only four years before his death.

To sketch briefly the remainder of the history of the NSR. By 1947 both locomotives were unserviceable and were sold for scrap two years later. A permanent arrangement had to be made of hiring from the LNER (and later from the North Eastern Region of BR). Various types of motive power were tried, the most successful being the Class Y7 0-4-0T, in particular No.68089. This was the last of the class to be built, in 1923, and also the last to be withdrawn, in 1952. When this engine went to Darlington in 1948 for overhaul, its duties were taken over for a few months by a most unlikely replacement, a L&YR 'Pug' 0-4-0ST, No.11217.

Operation, even under LNER management, appears to have been somewhat haphazard. By 1941 fly-shunting was resumed and a graphic account of its working appears in the *Railway Observer* for December of that year. The railway did not always run smoothly and the *RO* again records:

On a visit on 31 January 1949, no train was waiting at Chathill. 'The engine's failed; it's the first time it's done it for three months now. You'll have to get in the taxi.' At Seahouses Y7 68089 had blown a joint but was repaired to take a fish special to Chathill in the afternoon but this had 'winded' her and so the return in the evening was again by taxi – carrying 12 passengers in addition to several bags of mail.

Meanwhile, the condition of the track was getting steadily worse and closure became inevitable; it is to be noted that both goods and passenger traffic continued to the end.

Once more, the *RO* gives a lively account of the last day:

This independent line was closed from 27 October 1951. For the last three weeks of service the line was operated by Tweedmouth drivers, the regular one having left to take up other employment. The first and last services were of late operated by taxi, usually a large Austin. Friday and Saturday, 26 and 27 October, saw the removal of all stock to Chathill, including coach No.2 which was in a very bad state of repair.

About 4 pm Y7 0-4-0T 68089 (hired from the NE Region), proudly displaying its head board *Farne Islander*, left Seahouses shed to take its place on the train, composed of NS coaches Nos 1 and 3. Several members were present and took many photographs. Promptly at 4.20 with about 40 passengers on board the train left on its last journey, to the accompaniment of two dozen fog signals. Many people were waving hands and handkerchiefs, the driver replying with much use of the whistle. On arrival at North Sunderland most passengers left the train; here again fog signals were placed on the line to say farewell and from here right to Chathill small groups of people were to be seen saying farewell to the *Farne Islander*.

The arrival at Chathill was very quiet, the remaining passenger dismounted, 68089 propelled the coaches out to the loop, ran round, and returned them to the station.

A Heaton engine crew were waiting for 68089, and after an Up passenger and freight had passed this small 0-4-0T left en route to its new abode.

The 5.50 pm return to Seahouses was a taxi, eight passengers were waiting, and when it arrived it was a Ford 8 h.p. car (*sic*). This meant two trips, and three in the back of a Ford 'Eight' complete with cameras etc., was nowhere near as comfortable as North Sunderland travel.

This was not quite the end of the story. At the Annual General Meeting in Newcastle on 18 April 1952, it was resolved that the Company must go into liquidation and, in order to do this, it was decided that it should be registered under the Companies Act, which was done on 23 April. A winding-up order was made on 16 June. The Company never paid a dividend in all the sixty years of its existence and there was no return of capital to the shareholders, a record surely almost without equal in the whole of the history of British railways? The liquidator was released on 15 July 1960 and the Company was finally struck off the Stock Exchange Register on 25 July 1969.

25. Cawood looking towards the buffer stops. The line was still open for goods traffic. *Author*

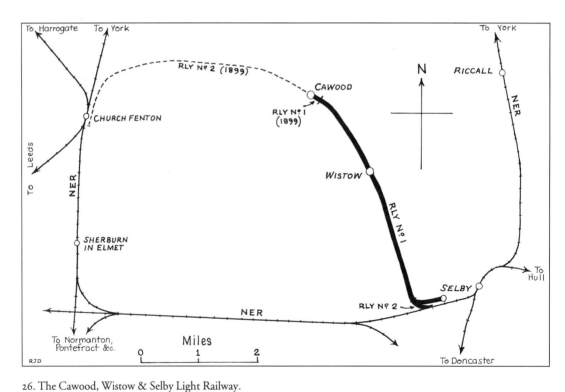

26. The Cawood, Wistow & Selby Light Railway.

CHAPTER FIVE

The Cawood, Wistow & Selby Light Railway

THE third railway with which Sebastian Meyer was associated was the Cawood, Wistow & Selby Light Railway. It was promoted by Meyer, Ben Day, Lt-Colonel T. G. Hawdon, Isaac White and Captain Henry Liversidge Jr. There was no opposition, the NER promising 'generous assistance'. It was incorporated on 2 July 1896 and, although the words 'Light Railway' appeared in its title, it was not built under the powers of the Light Railways Act, which was not passed until 14 August of that year. The Company obtained powers to construct Railway No.1, about 4½ miles long, from Broad Lane, Cawood, to near the Doncaster–Selby Road in Selby, and Railway No.2, a connecting line 160 yards in length, to form a junction with the Leeds & Selby Railway of the NER, 100 yards west of Brayton Gates signal box. This box then became known as 'Cawood Junction', later as 'Selby West' and, finally, as 'Selby'.

The authorised capital of the railway was £24,000 in £10 shares, with powers to raise a further £8,000 in Debentures.

This was not the first attempt to open up the district. In 1879, a railway titled the Church Fenton, Cawood & Wistow Railway was incorporated to build a line between those places. It obtained further powers in 1882 to extend eight miles to Drax to form a junction with the Hull & Barnsley Railway then being constructed. It changed its name in the following year to the Selby & Mid-Yorkshire Union Railway. The Company was supported by the H&BR whose Board regarded it as a means of access to Harrogate and to York. Three years later, the Company obtained an Act to

extend the time allowed for its construction. However, in 1889 it was permitted to abandon the section from Wistow to Drax and 1890 saw the complete abandonment of the scheme and the winding-up of the company.

The first directors of the Cawood Company were Captain Henry Liversidge Jr, Lt-Colonel Tom Gibson Hawdon and Isaac White, who had all been promoters of the Company. White was appointed Engineer, Ben Day the Solicitor, and D. C. Hartmann was Secretary *pro tem*. White, of course, was also Engineer to the E&WYUR. Day's name occurs frequently until the end of the story. Meyer became Manager and soon after incorporation he started to buy land for the railway, some of it in his own name which he later transferred to the Company. A small amount of land was rented. White resigned almost immediately from the Board; he may have felt that the two positions were not compatible. Captain C. F. Hoyle became a Director in his place.

At a Special General Meeting on 22 November 1897, with Ben Day in the chair, Philip Robert Meyer, Sebastian's younger brother, was appointed Secretary at a salary of £200 per annum. It was resolved that the whole of the authorised capital was to be divided into Preferred and Deferred half-shares, and that the dividend on the Preferred shares was to be four per cent.

The 'first sod' was cut at Cawood by Mrs Liversidge, wife of the Chairman, on 11 July 1896, only nine days after the passing of the Act.

Messrs Whitaker Brothers, of Horsforth, Leeds, were the contractors and, as there were no engineering difficulties, construction was rapid.

Goods traffic (according to the *Yorkshire Herald*, 'the conveyance of manures and other goods'; it is to be hoped not in the same wagons) started early, probably about the end of 1897. The line was inspected on 9 February 1898 by Colonel Addison, RE, one of the Board of Trade inspectors, and passed for passenger traffic. The railway was publicly opened by Alderman Edwin Gray, Lord Mayor of York and Under-Steward of the Manors of Wistow and Cawood, on 16 February. The official train, for which special tickets were issued, was booked to leave Brayton Gates Siding at 12.45. The *Yorkshire Herald* stated that 'substantial stations have been built at Selby, Wistow and Cawood'. A 'substantial' (this seems a favourite word of the reporter) public luncheon was held in the village school room at Wistow, tickets for which were 2s 6d. The guests included, among many others, William Hutchinson, JP, of Gunby near Selby, Sebastian's father-in-law, Sebastian and Philip Meyer, Ben Day, Edward Sisterson and Richard Smith, Secretary of the North Sunderland Railway.

At first a service of five trains each way per day was arranged, taking 17 minutes for the journey. The *Herald* stated that these were mixed trains but Hartley, in his book, says that mixed trains were not run.

At the General Meeting, on 16 August 1898, exactly six months after opening, with Captain Liversidge in the chair, it was decided to pay four per cent on the Preferred shares and three on the Deferred.

The following year was a momentous one for the Light Railway. At a Special Meeting on 14 January a draft Light Railway Order, under the Light Railways Act of 1896, was approved. This was for two railways, No.1 of which, 1fur 5ch long, was from the termination of the line at Broad Lane to Sherburn Road, Cawood. It would appear that this had already been constructed without authority (see below). Railway No.2 continued

beyond for 4 miles 1fur 5 ch, to end at the east side of Church Fenton station. No junction was specified but the Light Railway hoped to get a connection without asking for compulsory powers.

The proposal appears to have thoroughly alarmed the Board of the NER. It did not wish a repeat of the Selby & Mid-Yorkshire Union project, with the risk of a potentially dangerous penetrating line falling into hostile hands. The NER decided to purchase the smaller company for £32,000 as from 1 January 1899. This was public knowledge by March 1899. In April the NER Board decided that it would not proceed with the Church Fenton Order and, in June, it wrote to the Cawood Company that the latter was not to promote any new railway between Cawood and Church Fenton. It was agreed that the NER would pay interest from 1 January at the rate of four per cent, and that the Cawood Company would continue to pay the interest on the Debentures. The smaller company would carry on working the line as agents of the NER until the actual sale on 1 January 1900.

At the half-yearly meeting in February 1899, dividends of four per cent were declared on both the Preference and Deferred shares. D. S. Hartmann and William Close were auditors. Close was a Director of the Yorkshire Railway Wagon Co. Ltd of Wakefield and, later, one of the auditors of the Great Northern and the Dearne Valley Railway Companies.

A public inquiry into the proposed Cawood and Church Fenton extension was held in Selby on 14 July 1899, but the proceedings were something of a farce. The Cawood Company felt that it was policy to continue with their application. It was said that the railway would open up the district for agricultural traffic and that Selby was the natural market town for Church Fenton. The NER, knowing that it was about to purchase the Light Railway, raised no opposition. The Light Railway Commissioners stated that they had no hesitation

SELBY, WISTOW, and CAWOOD (Auto-cars—One class only).—North Eastern.													
Miles	**Down.**		**Week Days only.**					**Miles**	**Up.**		**Week Days only.**		
		mrn	mrn	aft		aft	aft		aft			mrn	mrn	aft	aft		aft
—	Selby ....dep.	8 31	1140	3 25		5 07	22	10 5	—	Cawood ......dep.	8 52		1053	12 53	52	7 44	1027
3¾	Wistow...........	8 42	1151	3 36		5 11	7 33	1016	1¾	Wistow...........	8 57		1058	1216	3 57	7 49	10 32
5¼	Cawood ......arr.	8 48	1157	3 42		5 17	7 39	1022	5¼	Selby 768, 770 arr.	9 9		1110	1222	4 9	8 1	1044

27. The Selby to Cawood timetable from the 1914 'Bradshaw'.

28. On 22 April 1960 a party toured the line in brake vans headed by
a diesel shunter, D2063. *R. B. Parr*

in recommending the Board of Trade to issue an
Order. After the hearing, the Commissioners travelled over the line on a special train. It was then
announced that the NER had acquired the CW&SLR
and the whole of the proposals before the Commissioners were withdrawn.

These arrangements were legalised by the NER
Act of 30 July 1900, which confirmed the sale of
the CW&SLR, as stated in an Agreement of 1 June
1899, and said that it was to be worked as a Light
Railway. The Act confirmed that some 300 yards
of railway at Cawood, 'already constructed',
should be considered as part of the Cawood
Railway authorised in 1896. A Schedule to the Act
transferred 'all rights and interest' in the Church
Fenton Extension to the NER.

The final meetings of the Cawood Company
took place on 27 February 1900, a General
Meeting followed immediately afterwards by a
Special Meeting. At both Sebastian Meyer was
Chairman, but unfortunately neither the official
minutes nor the newspaper reports state in what

capacity he was acting. At the first meeting the
accounts were approved and at the second a
resolution was passed to authorise the Directors to
support the NER Bill.

The independent existence of the Cawood
Railway ceased after some three years of private
operation. The Company may be said to have been
moderately successful, paying the promised four
per cent on its Preference shares and three and a
half to four on the Deferred.

The locomotive *Cawood* and two passenger
carriages, on hire purchase from the Yorkshire
Railway Wagon Co., were sold on 6 July 1901 for
£150 to the Yorkshire District Light Railway
Syndicate, of which more later, but the Syndicate
were to continue to pay the rentals to the hiring
company. Perhaps this was not such a bargain as was
once thought (see the author's *Railways of the South
Yorkshire Coalfield*, p.40). The locomotive was used
by the Syndicate on the construction of the Goole &
Marshland Light Railway. It was next acquired by
the Leeds Contract Co., another of Meyer's

29. Wistow station. *Author*

concerns, and used by them on the building of part of the North Lindsey Light Railway.

The railway was a single line worked by 'one engine in steam'. The line, passing through the flat countryside of the Vale of York, had few engineering features. A plate girder bridge, supported on brick piers, crossed the Selby Dam near the commencement of the railway. The Selby Dam is a once-navigable stream also crossed today by the Selby Diversion of the East Coast Main Line but on a much more substantial viaduct. There were seven level crossings; all were over minor roads, with the exception of the first one over the Selby–Leeds road, now the A63. The LNER Appendix for 1947 states that the gates at Flaxley Road, Selby Common and Broad Lane (Cawood), in the absence of a crossing keeper, were to be opened and closed by the trainmen. Presumably Leeds Road and Wistow were always manned. The other crossings were over country lanes. There were sidings at Leeds Road, Crosshills, Flaxley, Selby Common, 'Wistow Junction', and South Lane (Cawood).

The two stations at Wistow and Cawood were pleasant brick buildings, different in style from other NER rural stations, reflecting their separate origin. The crossing keepers' cottages and the goods sheds were also well built and, with some exceptions, are standing today.

After its acquisition by the NER, the Cawood branch settled down to a quiet existence. On 1 July 1904, Brayton Gates station at Selby was closed and the passenger services diverted to the main-line station. The NER appear to have regarded the line as a 'test-track' for experimental vehicles. One of their 'Petrol-Electric Autocars' was used for several years. A Leyland bus on rail-wheels went to the line in 1923 but it came to a fiery end, being completely burnt out later the same year in Selby shed. Sentinel railcars, Sentinel locomotives and, of course, ordinary small steam engines were used. Passenger services ceased on 1 January 1930 and goods traffic on 2 May 1960. A rail tour, using brake-vans hauled by diesel locomotive D2063, paid the enthusiasts' last respects on 27 April 1960.

CHAPTER SIX

The Dearne Valley
Railway

THE Dearne Valley Railway was promoted in
1896 by James Jenkin Addy, Managing
Director of Carlton Main and Grimethorpe
Collieries; Ernest Hague, Managing Director of
Hickleton Main Colliery and a Director of Manvers
Main; Charles E. Hunter of Houghton Main and
Manvers Main Collieries; and Robert Armitage, a
Director of Hickleton Main and other companies.
Like their colleagues in West Yorkshire, they were
dissatisfied with the rail facilities of the district,
especially to the ports of Grimsby and Hull,
provided by the Manchester, Sheffield & Lincoln-
shire and North Eastern Railways. Accordingly, a
Bill was deposited seeking powers to build a railway,
some 21 miles long, from junctions with the Hull &
Barnsley Railway near Brierley, through Grimethorpe, Houghton, Goldthorpe, Cadeby and Edlin-
ton, to junctions with the Great Northern Railway
and the Great Northern & Great Eastern Joint line
at respectively Black Carr and Bessacarr, Doncaster.
It was proposed to construct a dock or wharf on the
River Don at Mexborough, branches to various
collieries en route and two connections in the
direction of the Swinton & Knottingley Joint line. It
was stated that the line was projected by I. White
and S. W. Meyer, of Leeds.

The Act received Royal Assent on 6 August
1897, the same day as the neighbouring Hull &
South Yorkshire Extension Railway (later the
Wath branch of the H&BR). The railway, but not
the dock, was constructed much as authorised,
unlike the unfulfilled ambitions of the East &
West Yorkshire Union Railways. The junction at
Brierley was in a much simpler form than
originally planned but, as events turned out, traffic

in this direction was probably not nearly so great as
the promoters had hoped. The authorised capital
was £600,000, with borrowing powers for a
further £200,000. The railway was to be
completed in five years.

Earlier in the year a meeting of the promoters
had taken place at which S. W. Meyer was
appointed Secretary, Ben Day Solicitor and I. W.
H. White Engineer – the 'Old Firm' coming
together again. At that meeting it was resolved to
try to get rates from the H&BR for the carriage of
coal to Hull as favourable as those granted to the
South Yorkshire Junction Railway. The H&BR
desired to be friendly with the new Company but
it was unable to assist financially. The GER was
prepared to enter an Agreement on the lines of
their's with the Lancashire, Derbyshire & East
Coast Railway, but the promoters decided to try to
get more favourable terms from some other railway
company. In connection with this, and also with
regard to negotiations with the Great Northern
Railway, the services of Henry Lambert, formerly
General Manager of the Great Western Railway,
were obtained, no doubt on the advice of Meyer.
Lambert recommended independence from any of
the larger companies. In this year, it was decided
that the offices of the Company should be at 13
Bond Street, Leeds, which was also the offices of
the East & West Yorkshire Union Railways.
Meanwhile White wrote to the Lancashire &
Yorkshire Railway suggesting that the DVR be
extended to Horbury but the L&YR refused to co-
operate. At the same time meetings with the H&BR
were taking place.

In the following year, the tender of Messrs

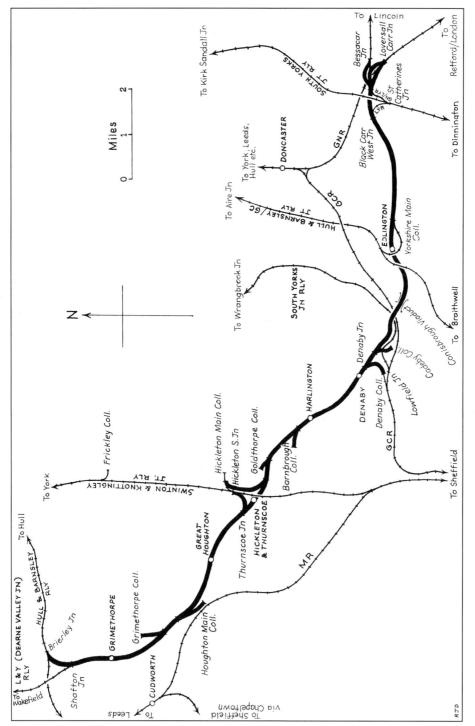

30. The Dearne Valley Railway

31. In spite of what it says on the box, this is Crofton Junction where the Dearne Valley Junction Railway diverged to the right from the L&YR's Wakefield (Kirkgate)–Goole line. Crofton East Junction, on the east facing curve, was just beyond the dismantled splitting signal. *M. A. King*

Naylor Brothers of Huddersfield was accepted for the first contract, from the H&BR at Brierley to Grimethorpe and Houghton Main Collieries. At the end of the year Lambert was paid 250 guineas (£262 50p) for his negotiations with the GNR.

The year 1899 was a busy one for the Company. The contract with Naylor Bros was sealed and they started work in August. A tender for the supply of rails from Edward Sisterson was accepted. It was proposed to make a junction with the Hull & South Yorkshire Extension Railway at Hickleton so that coal traffic from Manvers and Wath Collieries could be exchanged and that Company was approached to find out their terms for carriage. As this Company was acquired by the H&BR to form its Wath branch which served these collieries directly, it is not surprising that no more is heard of the proposal.

Another proposal, which also came to nothing, was for the L&YR to run from Barnsley over the Great Central (formerly MS&LR) Houghton Main branch to Houghton Main and Grimethorpe Collieries. The collieries again suggested connection to the L&YR, either via Barnsley or via Horbury.

In August it was reported that White was ill and he was unable to attend the Board meeting (he died in the December). It was considered that his charges were excessive. Next month, Stanley R. Kay, of the same firm, attended on his behalf; it was decided that £2,000 be offered to White and Kay jointly for their work on the first contract, which they accepted. At the same meeting, the Secretary's salary was fixed at £200 per annum.

At the end of the year Kay was appointed Engineer. Notice was received from the promoters of the Tickhill Light Railway that they proposed to make a junction with the DVR at St Catherine's. Addy, as Chairman of the DVR, was instructed to give evidence in support of the Light Railway.

The year 1900 was a crucial one for the Company. Contract No.2 from Houghton Main to a junction with the Swinton & Knottingley Joint line at Hickleton South was again awarded to Naylor Bros. The North Eastern Railway intimated that it wished to run to Houghton and Grimethorpe Collieries, on the same terms as the

The Conisbrough Viaduct
– chief engineering feature of the DVR.

32. *above:* The viaduct under construction.
Doncaster Central Library

33. *left:* The viaduct shortly after completion in 1909.
The central span is over the River Don Navigation.
Doncaster Central Library

34. *below* A rail tour traverses the viaduct westbound
on 11 May 1952. *C. Ord*

35. Passenger facilities were indeed primitive. This is the 'rebuilt' halt at Grimethorpe. Note the new brickwork and stairs. *Author*

H&BR, when this section had been completed.

It was a year of intense activity in negotiation with the L&YR conducted by Addy, Lambert and Meyer. In the end, it was hammered out that the L&YR would build a connecting line from Crofton to Shafton but, if the L&YR did not construct it, then the DVR would; the DVR was to have running powers over it for passenger traffic to Wakefield. The L&YR was to have full running powers to Black Carr. Mr Aspinall, General Manager of the L&YR, made a condition that, if the DVR did not work the line themselves, then the L&YR would have the first option to work or purchase the line. Meyer and Lambert demurred but Aspinall insisted. The agreement to purchase on three months' notice was confidential and a closely guarded secret. It was also agreed that the DVR would extend to Cadeby at the same time as the connecting line was being constructed. The L&YR promised to subscribe £200,000, i.e. one-third of the authorised capital, they would nominate two Directors to the Board, one of whom would be Chairman, and the L&YR would have control of the line. The L&YR would work the DVR for sixty per cent of the gross receipts. In November, the tender of Edward Sisterson for

300 tons of 'slightly defective rails' for use in sidings was approved.

The L&YR (Dearne Valley Junction Railways) Act of 26 July 1901 authorised the connecting line and allowed the raising of a further £246,000, with borrowing powers of £82,000. The L&YR laid down that the DVR was to grant no further running powers. It also stated that the DVR would find a shunting engine or hire one from the L&YR.

The DVR was opened from Brierley Junction to Grimethorpe and Houghton Main Collieries on 19 March 1902. In July the DVR purchased a 12-ton brake-van from the Birmingham Wagon Co., believed to have been the only vehicle the railway possessed. Meyer was now styled Secretary and Manager at a salary of £300 per annum and this would continue until the Crofton branch was opened. Then the managerial and secretarial work would be transferred to the L&YR and the Head Office would be at Hunts Bank, Manchester, but the Registered Office of the Company remained at 13 Bond Street, Leeds until the end. Meanwhile the quarterly meetings of the Board would be held alternately in Leeds and Manchester.

It was later decided that Meyer would remain as

36. Yorkshire Main Sidings Box, one of the numerous block posts controlling junctions with colliery lines, looking east on 10 October 1970. *M. A. King*

Secretary, at £150 a year. Kay would continue with the plans up to Denaby, but Mr Worthington, Chief Engineer of the L&YR, would take over from that point to Black Carr.

The L&YR Company's Act of July 1902 granted it the necessary powers to subscribe to the DVR and, at the first Board meeting after that, on 14 October, Sir George Armitage, Chairman of the L&YR, took his place as Chairman of the DVR. E. B. Fielden was their other nominee; J. J. Addy became Deputy-Chairman.

At the end of the year it was agreed that the DVR would hire an engine from the L&YR to work exclusively on the line for £15 a week, the DVR paying the driver and fireman and providing coal. General merchandise would be dealt with at Grimethorpe and Houghton stations and the L&YR would provide the wagons. The H&BR intimated

that it wished to exercise its running powers to the collieries, but was informed that this could not be done with safety until signalling was fully installed.

It was reported that Contract No.2, to Hickleton, was completed by 4 August 1903 but that section was not opened until 13 March 1905. Contract No.3, from Thurnscoe to Denaby, was awarded to Gates & Hogg, of Doncaster. Kay was to be paid three per cent of £115,017, the price of the contract, and also a similar amount for the previous one.

J. W. Close was appointed Accountant in 1904. By the end of 1905, only £332,000 of the authorised capital had been paid up. The subscribers were the L&YR Co. (£200,000), Carlton Main and Grime-thorpe, and Houghton Main (£56,000 each), Hickleton Main (£14,000), and £1,000 each by C. E. Hunter (Houghton Main), R. Armitage

(Hickleton), J. Jarrett (Houghton), the executors of E. Hague (Hickleton), T. E. Vickers and J. J. Addy (both of Carlton Main and Grimethorpe Collieries).

The DVR Act of 30 June 1905 allowed the Company to issue £110,000 (i.e. roughly one-third of the paid-up capital) in four per cent Debenture shares. The L&YR took £109,000 of these in the name of some of the Directors of the Company, as it had no powers to subscribe any further money to the DVR. J. Jarrett took up the odd £1,000. During 1906 the L&YR subscribed to further Ordinary, Preference and Debenture shares, making a grand total of £477,000. The final contract from Denaby to Black Carr and Bessacarr was awarded in October 1904 to H. Lovatt & Co., of Wolverhampton, for £175,300. This included the massive Conisbrough viaduct across the valley of the Don. This contract was marred by a number of fatal accidents. In March 1906 three workmen were killed and two seriously injured when one of them hit a charge of gelignite at Loversall Road, near Balby. In December a navvy, riding on an engine, was fatally scalded through the bursting of a boiler tube and, about the same time, a man fell off Conisbrough viaduct.

The section from Thurnscoe to Cadeby was opened on 8 January 1906, the coal traffic from Denaby and Cadeby Collieries being worked by the contractors, Gates & Hogg, until the L&YR took over on 4 August 1906. The railway was finally completed by 17 May 1909, including Conisbrough viaduct and the junctions with the South Yorkshire Joint line and at Black Carr and Bessacarr.

The railway settled down to its main business of carrying coal, but, in November 1911, the General Manager suggested that 'a Rail Motor service of Steam Cars' should be commenced and he recommended the provision of five halts at a cost of £583. This was approved, and the *Yorkshire Post* for 22 May 1912 carried the advertisement:

From 24 May 1912. The L&YR and DVR are about to co-operate in running a service of RAIL MOTOR CARS between Wakefield (L&Y) and Edlington. Halts are provided at Ryhill, Grimethorpe, Great Houghton and Harlington but there are no stations on the line as it is not adapted for the running of ordinary passenger trains, but an endeavour is being made by the two companies referred to, to afford some travelling

facilities to the inhabitants of the district. The service, however, did not commence until 3 June. A sixth halt was opened at Denaby on 1 December 1913.

In 1913 a Dearne Valley Light Railway was proposed. This was a street tramway linking Barnsley, Thurnscoe, Swinton and Manvers. It was opposed by the DVR, not so much on the grounds of competition, but because of possible confusion in the title. The Solicitor was instructed to take steps to get the name of the scheme changed. It is not recorded if the 'steps' were amicable but the result was that the tramway became the Dearne District Light Railways. (The tram line was not opened until 1924 and closed in 1933, a very short life.)

The General Manager of the DVR, now Arthur Watson, advised the Board in 1920 that passenger traffic did not average more than nine per train and this did not warrant the provision of shelters. Nevertheless, a year later he reported that a deputation had been received from the local authorities for some form of shelter at the various halts. 'There was no form of shelter of any kind at the present time and, having regard to the building operations now going on in the district, he recommended that an old carriage body should be made suitable and fixed at each halt at about £95, or approximately £570 for the six halts.' These were duly provided and they lasted until the line closed to passenger trains on 10 September 1951.

Meyer's salary was increased in 1920 to £200 per annum and he was given the title of Secretary and Accountant, no doubt taking on the duties of the late J. W. Close. Early in 1922, Meyer reported that the amalgamation of the Lancashire & Yorkshire and the London & North Western Railways had taken place. The Dearne Valley Company was merged into the enlarged LNWR in November 1922, its last meeting taking place at Euston on the 23rd. The holders of Ordinary stock received £100 in cash for each £100 held and the four per cent Debenture owners were given £133 6s 8d in three per cent LNWR Debentures for each £100. Many of the shares were cancelled as they were already owned by the 'taking-over' company. The DVR had been reasonably prosperous, paying dividends of about 2¼ to 2¾ per cent.

S. W. Meyer received £2,500 compensation for loss of office.

37. The abandoned flyover across the East Coast main line in 1973 before reinstatement. *Author*

38. The South Yorkshire Junction line bridge over the Dearne Valley at Black Carr West in 1973, with the GNR bridge (now demolished) beyond. *Author*

39. The GNR bridge (now demolished) at Black Carr West, 1973. *Author*

40. A similar view after reinstatement. This line is now electrified and signalled for bi-directional working. *Author*

41. Black Carr East. The bridge over the East Coast main line is beyond the crane. The flyover, now demolished, over the GN&GE Joint line is in the background. 1975. *Author*

42. Black Carr East Junction, now Flyover East Junction. The connections with the up East Coast main line to the right, the GN&GE Joint line to Lincoln on the left. A 1975 view. *Author*

43. The abandoned DVR main line, now a nature reserve, with the South Yorkshire Joint line bridge in the Background. *Author*

DESCRIPTION OF THE LINE

As the Dearne Valley Railway was not a Light Railway, it was built and worked to main-line standards. Originally it was single line, controlled by Electric Tablet and fully signalled. The DVR proper started from a conventional double junction with the Hull & Barnsley Railway at Brierley. It quickly expanded into a fan of exchange sidings, situated in a cutting, which contracted into a single line before joining the Dearne Valley Junction Railway from Crofton, at Shafton Junction. There were detailed instructions to the Joint Shunter at the sidings and the signalman at Shafton for the working of trains over this single-line section. Between 1912 and 1915 the line was doubled from Shafton Junction to Barnburgh Colliery and for about a mile between Denaby Halt and Cadeby. These sections were worked by Permissive Block. Beyond Black Carr West Junction the railway was double track or wider.

Signal boxes, generally to serve colliery junctions, were placed at Shafton Junction, Hodroyd Colliery, Grimethorpe Sidings, Houghton Sidings, Thurnscoe Junction, Nicholas Lane, Hickleton Colliery Sidings, Goldthorpe Colliery, Barnborough (*sic*), Denaby Sidings and Halt, Yorkshire Main Sidings, Black Carr West Sidings, and Black Carr East Sidings.

There were branches to serve the collieries, which were mostly worked by 'one engine in steam'; to Grimethorpe Colliery; to Houghton Main Colliery; and a double line connection to the Swinton & Knottingley Joint line at Hickleton Main Colliery Sidings (which allowed the NER access to Houghton and Grimethorpe). At Denaby there were branches to Denaby Main Colliery, the final 21 chains of which belonged to the L&YR, and a branch to Cadeby Main Colliery. The DVR was connected to Yorkshire Main Colliery near Edlington Halt. There were curves to the South Yorkshire Joint Railway, from Black Carr West and

44. In LMS days and ex-L&YR steam railcar waits its turn of duty over the DVR at Wakefield (Kirkgate). *G. J. Aston*

45. In BR days a 'rail-motor train' headed by a Stanier 2-6-2 T pauses at Goldthorpe & Thurnscoe Halt. *Doncaster Central Library*

East to St Catherine's, the western one being L&YR-owned and the eastern one L&Y and GNR Joint. Finally, the LMSR put in a line to serve Rossington Colliery. This was worked by 'one engine in steam' but a token was used in place of the usual staff. A flat crossing with a colliery line was protected by a crossbar signal, a rare thing at this late date.

There were many engineering features on the line, the first of which was a short tunnel south of Shafton Junction. The railway passed through a cutting near Harlington which was followed by an embankment some two and a half miles long over ground which was subject to flooding from the River Dearne, which was crossed twice. (The river has subsequently in the 1960s been diverted and straightened, lessening that risk.) The railway turned into the valley of the Don and ran in a cutting in the hillside. For a short distance the DVR, the South Yorkshire Junction Railway (worked by the H&BR), the Denaby and Cadeby Colliery lines, the main Great Central Sheffield to Doncaster line, the Don itself (canalised as the Sheffield & South Yorkshire Navigation), and the Mexborough to Conisbrough highway were all running parallel through the valley. The DVR was soon carried over the SYJR and it then crossed the GCR, which was in its Conisbrough tunnel. After this, the railway crossed the well-known Conisbrough viaduct, 1,525 feet long and 113 feet above the river; strangely, this was at a summit on the line. There were twenty-one brick arches and a steel lattice-girder bridge with a span of 150 feet over the river. At the present time, there have been many suggestions to use the viaduct as a road bridge across the valley but its only use in that direction is for dumper-trucks carrying quarry spoil for disposal elsewhere.

After the viaduct the railway entered another limestone cutting, seventy feet deep, where originally a tunnel had been planned. At Black Carr East Junction, the DVR terminated in two flying

46. An excursion train at the same location as fig 45. *Author*

junctions: the first, to the GNR main line at Loversall Carr, crossed that railway on an imposing skew lattice-girder bridge carrying double track; the second connection was to the GN&GE Joint line at Bessacarr, the Up line of which crossed the joint line on a similar but smaller single-line girder bridge, now demolished.

The ruling gradient, except for one short stretch at Goldthorpe, was 1 in 100 but, as the coal trains were heavy, powerful locomotives had to be used.

The DVR ran against the grain as far as other railways in the area were concerned, so crossings with other lines were numerous. The first was over the Great Central & Midland Joint line to Grimethorpe Colliery. This was followed by the DVR bridging over the Swinton & Knottingley Railway and almost immediately after this the H&BR Wath branch crossed over. Near Cadeby the DVR, as mentioned, crossed the SYJR and the GCR main line. At Warmsworth the H&B & GCR Joint line, and a branch off this to Yorkshire Main Colliery, crossed over the DVR on separate bridges. At Black Carr West, closely together, the DVR passed under a GNR spur from the South Yorkshire Joint line to Decoy Sidings and then the South Yorkshire Joint line itself. The final crossings have been described.

WAKEFIELD (KIRKGATE) AND EDLINGTON FOR BALBY (ONE CLASS ONLY). (DONCASTER).								Table 191

Left — WEEK DAYS ONLY.

						SO	SO	
Wakefield (Kirkgate) ....dep.	8 10	10 25	1 5	3 50	5 45	8 15	10 6	...
Ryhill	8 29	10 44	1 24	4 9	6 4	8 34	10 25	...
Grimethorpe	8 37	10 52	1 32	4 17	6 12	8 42	10 33	...
Great Houghton	8 47	11 2	1 42	4 27	6 22	8 52	10 43	...
Goldthorpe and Thuruscoe	8 52	11 7	1 47	4 32	6 27	8 57	10 48	...
Harlington	8 58	11 13	1 53	.	6 33	.	.	...
Denaby for Conisboro' & Mexboro'	9 2	11 17	1 57	.	6 37	.	.	...
Edlington for Balby ....arr. (Doncaster)	9 10	11 25	2 5	.	6 45	.	.	...

Right — WEEK DAYS ONLY.

						SO	SO
Edlington for Balby ....dep. (Doncaster)	9 18	11 33	2 13	...	6 50	...	...
Denaby, for Conisboro' & Mexboro'	9 26	11X44	2 23	.	6X59	.	.
Harlington	9 33	11 49	2 28	.	7 4	.	.
Goldthorpe and Thuruscoe	9 40	11 55	2 34	4 40	7 17	9 5	10 57
Great Houghton	9 45	12 0	2 39	4 45	7 22	9 10	11 2
Grimethorpe	9 56	12 11	2 50	4 56	7 33	9 21	11 13
Ryhill	10 5	12 20	2 59	5 5	7 42	2 29	11 22
Wakefield (Kirkgate) ....arr.	10 21	12 36	3 15	5 22	7 59	9 45	11 38

SO – Saturdays only.   X—Arrives Denaby 11.41 a.m., 2.21 and 6.58 p.m. respectively.   Y Arrives 7.9 p.m.

47. Timetable for the Wakefield–Balby line, July 1939.

CHAPTER SEVEN

The Brackenhill Light Railway and the
Yorkshire District Light Railway Syndicate

THE Brackenhill Light Railway was mooted early in 1896 by some of the quarry owners at Ackworth Moor Top. They proposed a line from their freestone quarries to the West Riding & Grimsby Railway near Hemsworth station. Henry Oakley, the manager of the GNR, was approached and he replied that the matter would receive his company's attention. (The GNR were joint owners with the MS&LR of the WR&GR.) The *Pontefract Express*, in January 1896, reported that the GNR surveyors were taking measurements and said, 'Whether it will only be for heavy traffic, and not passengers, it is premature to say.'

Plans were deposited in 1898 for a railway, No.1, from the north side of the GNR (*sic*), near Hemsworth station (no compulsory junction was requested), to the Wakefield–Doncaster road, about two miles in length, with two branches, Nos 2 and 3, both about half a mile long, to quarries at Brackenhill and Ackworth Moor Top. Included in the draft Light Railway Order were proposals for the incorporation of the Yorkshire District Light Railway Syndicate Ltd 'which are united into a Company for the purpose of making and maintaining the Railway'. The *Railway Times* of 25 March 1899 had said that the Company was 'recently formed to promote, construct, purchase or take on lease any railway, tramway, or any works, rolling stock or materials in connection therewith, any lands, properties, estates and effects, or any grants, concessions, leases or other interests, and to build and maintain, gas, water, and electric works, telegraph or telephone systems, as company promoters' – a fairly comprehensive order. The capital was £50,000, and the first directors were

Isaac White, Sebastian William Meyer, Ben Day and Edward Sisterson. The offices of the Syndicate were in Leeds.

Ben Day was the Solicitor to the railway company, and Isaac White, of Messrs Mammatt & White, the Engineer. The estimated cost of construction of the line was £21,779.

A Public Inquiry was held at the Bull Hotel, Wakefield, on 27 September 1899 before the Light Railway Commissioners, the Earl of Jersey and Colonel Boughey. Counsel for the Light Railway said the purpose of the line was to carry stone, at present taken by traction engines or carts, to the GNR at Hemsworth. The proposed capital was £24,000. Meyer, as Manager of the YDLRS, said the Syndicate had promoted lines in East and West Yorkshire and one or two others. He was consulted, as the representative of the Syndicate, by the owners of some fourteen quarries. S. R. Kay, a member of White's firm, also gave evidence; no doubt Mr White was too ill to attend.

There was strong opposition from the New Hemsworth Colliery Co. and from Earl Fitzwilliam who owned most of the land the railway wished to acquire. Their Counsel stated that the proposal did nothing for the colliery which was the most important industry in the district and that they were considering a line to the North Eastern Railway (*sic* to the Swinton & Knottingley Joint line of the Midland and the NER was meant) but the Light Railway would interfere with this.

After an adjournment, the opposition was withdrawn, as the promoters agreed to apply in November for an extension to the Swinton & Knottingley Joint Railway and to give the colliery a

61

satisfactory connection and siding. The Commissioners approved the Order subject to an application for an extension being made.

A further Public Inquiry was held in Wakefield on 5 March 1900, the same day and place as an application from the E&WYUR. The Commissioners were Mr G. Fitzgerald and Colonel Boughey. This was for new lines from the New Hemsworth colliery to Railway No.1 of 1898, a quarter of a mile long, and from this railway to the S&KJt, south of Ackworth, 1¾ miles long; the estimated cost of these was £26,423. This time, there was no serious opposition, the Colliery Company now being entirely in favour. Opposition came from the owner of Moor House Farm, Ackworth, who said the embankment would interfere with hunting (an old story) and spoil his view, and he suggested an alternative route. Mr Meyer, who said he was not a railway engineer, replied that his route was the only one possible if the line were to be made at reasonable cost. It was now to be a mineral line to provide facilities to the Colliery Company for the carriage of coal to Goole

and Hull. The Syndicate, however, proposed to take powers to run one or two passenger trains a day to Pontefract. The representatives of the local authorities pressed for this.

The Commissioners considered the question of passenger services was of great importance and they proposed to postpone their decision until such an undertaking was given.

Satisfactory arrangements must have been made as the Board of Trade granted the Light Railway Order on 19 March 1901. This authorised Railway No.1 from Hemsworth to the Wakefield – Doncaster road, No.2 to Brackenhill, No.3 to Ackworth Moor Top, No.4 from New Hemsworth Colliery to Railway No.1, and No.5 to a junction with the S&KJt at Ackworth. The Company might construct a junction with the sidings at Hemsworth station, and could make Working Arrangements with the GN, Mid, GC, NE and/or WR&G Railways. The authorised capital was £54,000, with borrowing powers of £18,000. Of this, only £1,250 was issued as ordinary shares, not to the general public,

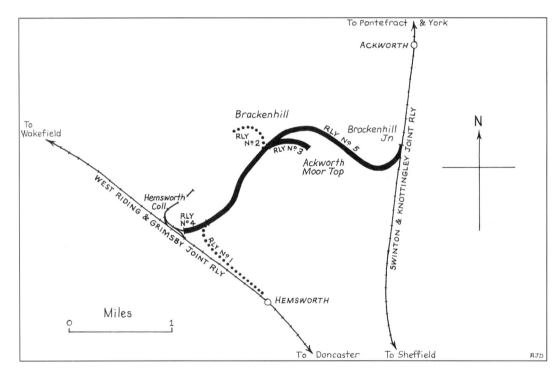

48. The Bracken Hill Light Railway

49. The Brackenhill Light Railway at Hemsworth Colliery. The ex-GNR Doncaster–Wakefield–Leeds line is in the background. *P. Cookson*

but to Messrs Sebastian Meyer, Day, Sisterson, Hartmann, George Parish and Philip Meyer.

This Light Railway Order also incorporated the Yorkshire District Light Railway Syndicate, which appears to have been carrying out its activities unofficially.

The first meeting of the Directors of the Light Railway took place on 21 March 1901; they were Sebastian Meyer (Chairman), Sisterson, Day, Hartmann and Philip Meyer. The last was appointed Secretary. Six months later they resigned and all were re-elected except Philip Meyer, who was now ineligible on his appointment as Secretary.

Nothing was done in the way of construction and an Order granting an extension of time was sanctioned on 22 September 1904. In spite of a promised output of a million tons of coal a year from the colliery, it was affected by labour troubles and went into liquidation. The colliery company was purchased by the South Kirkby & Featherstone Main Collieries in 1906.

Still nothing was done and it was necessary to apply for another extension of time, which was granted by the Board of Trade, without further Local Inquiry, on 16 April 1907, for four more years. The promoters stated that the colliery company was strongly in favour of the line but that they, the promoters, would be unable to raise the money until the market was normal and they had a guarantee of traffic from the colliery.

Early in 1909 the North Eastern Railway was expressing an interest in the Light Railway. The NER Board resolved to purchase it for £5,000 and to obtain Parliamentary sanction for the transfer of the Order. An Extraordinary General Meeting of the proprietors of the Brackenhill Light Railway approved the Bill for vesting their Company in the NER. The capital of the Light Railway was to be transferred to five of the Directors of the NER, as trustees for that Company, and they would become Directors of the Brackenhill company until the purchase was approved by Parliament. On 28 July 1909 all the Directors of the Light Railway resigned and were replaced by J. L. Wharton, Lord Wenlock, Viscount Ridley, Sir Hugh Bell and Sir George S. Gibb, all Directors of the NER; Philip Meyer's position as Secretary was confirmed at a salary of £25 per annum.

The NER Bill of 1910–11 included powers to authorise the transfer but, owing to the opposition of the GCR and the GNR, this part of the Bill was struck out. The Act, however, granted a further extension of time for another five years. The Brackenhill Light Railway remained a nominally independent line until it was absorbed into the LNER in the 1923 Grouping and its Directors continued to be Directors of the NER. The last meeting of the Company took place on 24 February 1923 when Philip Robert Meyer was still Secretary.

The NER lost no time. Tenders were invited in May 1911 and that of Thomas Wrigley, of Manchester, for £33,251 12s 4d, was accepted. It will be noted that, although the Yorkshire District Light Railway Syndicate was specially formed to construct the Brackenhill line, in fact it did not do so and all its activities were elsewhere. It maintained a dormant existence until it disappeared from the Leeds directories about 1910. The last reference traced to it is a payment in 1911 by the NER of £1,250, the amount spent in obtaining the Order of 1901.

In 1913 Colonel J. R. Shaw, Managing Director of the South Kirkby, Featherstone & Hemsworth Collieries, said that colliers would be able to travel on the new railway, to be opened in April 1914, between Hemsworth and Pontefract (Baghill). The railway was, in fact, opened for goods and mineral traffic on 1 July 1914 from Hemsworth Colliery to Brackenhill Junction, Ackworth, with a short branch to Ackworth Moor Top goods station. The section to Hemsworth station was not built. It is not known if miners' 'Paddy' trains ever ran; certainly the promised public passenger service never materialised.

Wrigley reported in 1916 that he had made a loss of £9,000 on the contract and the NER made an extra payment of £2,500 to him.

The line was really an ordinary goods branch of the NER. It was agreed that all traffic to the north should be worked by the NER, and that to the south would be worked to Ackworth station by the NER where it could be handed over to other companies. The branch closed on 1 January 1962.

The line was single, worked by 'one engine in steam'. There was a cutting at Ackworth Moor Top, followed by an overline bridge carrying the Doncaster to Wakefield road; the promoters had hoped to cross this by a level crossing but the Light Railway Commissioners overruled this. The railway was mostly in cutting from Brackenhill to Ackworth but this has now been filled in and landscaped. It passed under the Barnsley to Pontefract road and into a steep-sided rock cutting. The next section was fairly steeply graded, with a descent of 1 in 87 down to Mill Lane, and there are stories of loaded coal trains, whistling madly, dashing across the road, but fortunately without loss of life or serious injury. Beyond this the embankment has largely been removed and the land returned to agriculture. The branch joined the S&KJT line at Brackenhill Junction.

50. Ackworth Moor
Top goods depot.
P. Cookson

CHAPTER EIGHT

The Axholme Light Railways

THE Goole & Marshland Light Railway was proposed in 1896, the promoters being H. T. Bennett, Benjamin Clegg, William Coulman, Frederick J. Dupois, Edward Clark Foster and William Halkon, who were all members of the Goole Farmers' Club. Plans were deposited for lines from a triangular junction with the NER's Hull and Doncaster line to Adlingfleet with branches to Swinefleet and Luddington, having a total length of about 13½ miles. The Engineers were Mammatt and White. A public inquiry was held in the Lowther Hotel, Goole, before the Light Railway Commissioners, the Earl of Jersey and Colonel Boughey, on Saturday 7 October 1897.

It was said that there were no engineering difficulties; several warping drains had to be crossed, but, with the exception of the Swinefleet Warping Drain, they were of no great importance. The landowners were in favour; some had given the land and others were only asking agricultural values for it. Potatoes were the staple crop of the district.

White estimated the cost at about £4,236 per mile, or a total of £59,600. Agreements had been reached with the NER Company. The Commissioners stated that it was a case in which a Light Railway would be of great benefit to the owners and occupiers of the district and that they would have great pleasure in recommending to the Board of Trade that an Order be made. The Light Railway Order was approved on 16 August 1898, one of the earliest to be granted.

A Directors' meeting on 2 September 1898, with Halkon in the Chair, confirmed Mammatt and White as Engineers and an Agreement was signed with Sebastian William Meyer and Isaac White for the construction of the line. The 'first sod' was cut on 22 September by Halkon, using an inscribed silver spade, before a large gathering at Mr Bramhill's farm at Boltgate, Eastoft. A bottle of champagne was broken over the hole. Meyer represented the Contractors (he is referred to as one of the Engineers in the newspaper reports), but White was unable to be present, probably on account of illness. After the ceremony the company adjourned to the farm house where many and varied toasts were honoured. Meyer made a long speech in which he spoke of the success of the Cawood line. But his most important statement was that heavier rails and chairs would be laid, suitable for NER engines.

The first meeting of shareholders took place in February 1899. Directors were appointed. They were Halkon, Bennett, Clegg, Coulman, Foster and George Thompson. The Secretary was Harry Hobson of Swinefleet. It was confirmed that Agreements had been signed with the NER and that a signal box had been erected at the junction. It was built at the expense of the Light Railway Company and the junction was nearer to Goole than shown in the Deposited Plans.

At the Directors' meeting that month it was reported that White and Meyer had made an application for payment for work already done, amounting to £1,000. Fully paid-up shares to that amount were issued to them in accordance with their Agreement. Further issues of shares were made to them during the year. In July shares to the value of £3,500 were issued to the Yorkshire District Light Railway Syndicate as assignees of

Meyer and White, at the first meeting of the Syndicate in connection with the Light Railway. Philip Robert Meyer was appointed Traffic Manager as a salary of £100 per annum. Debentures for £5,000 at 4 per cent, redeemable at 102 in five years time were issued to the Contractors in September.

The line was opened for goods traffic on 8 January 1900 from Marshland Junction to Reedness. In June the Directors inspected the line by train as far as it had been constructed. It was expected that the railway would be open to Fockerby by the end of the year. At this time the Light Railway was worked by the Contractors' locomotives, as there was a NER directive that the Marshland locomotives must not pass the junction unless authorised to do so.

The *Doncaster Gazette* of 11 November 1900 reported that negotiations had taken place by which the NER would take over the Goole & Marshland and the Isle of Axholme Light Railways. 'This means the Light Railways will be light no longer. They have, as a matter of fact, been constructed as

heavy lines and are capable of carrying a heavy mineral traffic. The Goole & Marshland will, as far as the traffic of its own immediate district is concerned, remain a largely agricultural line. The Isle of Axholme, which will connect with it at Reedness Junction will be a mineral line as well as an agricultural one'

Friday 4 January 1901 was marred by a head-on collision between two of the contractors' locomotives in thick fog near Eastoft. The locomotives involved were *Halkon* and *Elgie* (named after Ellen Grace, the daughter of Sebastian Meyer). The tubes of the latter engine burst, killing the driver and fireman. The accident is fully described in the author's *Railways of the South Yorkshire Coalfield* (pp.38/40).

The Directors inspected the line again in June as far as Fockerby and noted that the stations were almost completed. An Agreement for the purchase of the G&M for £70,000 by the NER was sealed by the Marshland Company on 20 January 1901, the sum to be paid on 1 October of that year and the

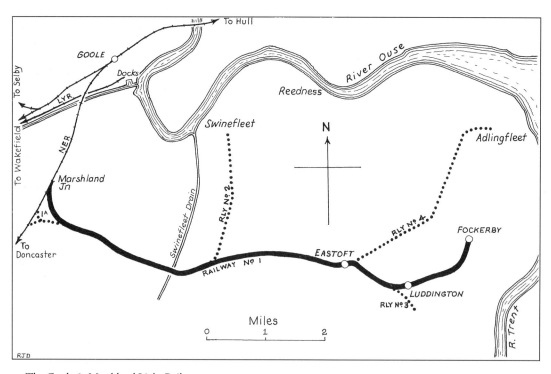

51. The Goole & Marshland Light Railway

52. Eastoft looking west.
D. Thompson

debentures to be paid off at 102. A special meeting of the shareholders of the G&M on 2 March 1901 confirmed the Agreement to sell to the NER and the following month there was a Town's Meeting in Goole in support.

The final Agreement with the NER and L&YR Companies was sealed on 11 June 1902 and the last meeting of the Directors took place on 1 October. In the end the price paid was £73,500 and the 4 per cent Debentures were paid off. The vesting was confirmed by the NER Act of 31 July 1902, effective from 2 October 1901. Interest at 4 per cent was to be paid on any outstanding balance by the two new owning companies. Philip Meyer was paid £100 'on the termination of his services as Secretary and Superintendent of the Goole & Marshland Railway'.

The Isle of Axholme Light Railway was promoted in 1897 to construct about twenty miles of railway from the GN&GE Joint Line at Haxey to the G&MLR at Reedness Junction. From the main line there was to be a connection to the Joint line at Haxey; branches from Epworth to Hatfield Moor and to Newlands and connections to the Sheffield & South Yorkshire Navigation and to the MSLR at Crowle. The line was to be primarily an agricultural one.

There had been many earlier proposals to make railways in the district. One of the first was the Direct

Northern of 1845, which would have run from London to York, passing through Walkeringham, Misterton, Owston and Haxey, thence to the east of Doncaster. In 1846 the Great Northern Railway Company proposed their Isle of Axholme Extension Railway which was to have run from Gainsborough and through Misterton, Haxey, Epworth, Crowle and Thorne. At that place it would have divided, the main line continuing to the authorised Doncaster to York line and a branch would have joined that line and the L&Y near Askern Junction. It was authorised in 1848, but not constructed.

Another proposal of 1846 was the Axholme, Gainsborough & Goole, like the York & North Midland one of George Hudson's strategic blocking lines. This was to have run from Selby through Rawcliff, Crowle, Haxey and Misterton to join another of Hudson's proposed lines near Gainsborough. Robert Stephenson was one of the Engineers, but it failed to get Parliamentary approval.

A later proposal was the Isle of Axholme & Marshland Tramway, a 3ft 6in tramway running from Haxey to Crowle, 'to be worked by animal, steam or any mechanical power, with the consent of the Board of Trade'. This was sanctioned in 1882. The Isle of Axholme & Marshland Steam Tramway Company was registered in June 1883, with a capital of £80,000 in £10 shares, to take over the powers granted by the Order of 1882. The MSLR

53. Luddington facing
west in June 1958.
D. Thompson

gained control of the Steam Tramway Company in August 1883 and this enabled it to oppose successfully the Goole, Epworth and Owston Railway, another scheme of 1882 for a line from Old Goole, and a junction with the NER south of Goole, to the Bawtry & Trent Railway & Dock, which had been sanctioned in that year. The Isle of Axholme Railway Act of 1885 permitted the abandonment of the Tramway and authorised a railway from Haxey to a junction with the MSLR at Crowle, no doubt with that Company's blessing. This in turn was abandoned by Act of 1888.

The Light Railway Act of 1896 provided the greatest opportunity for the construction of railways in the comparatively underdeveloped parts of the country such as the Isle of Axholme. Accordingly an application was heard before the Light Railway Commissioners at the Moot Hall, Crowle on 4 February 1898 for the construction of the Isle of Axholme Light Railway. The Directors were Thomas J. Blaydes, Henry Belcher, Edwin Hirst and up to six others. The first witness was Major George Dove, Chairman of the British Moss Litter Works Ltd, a name appearing many times later in this narrative. The engineer was Isaac White, who estimated the cost of the line at £133,000. There was no opposition from the main line companies, the GNR and the GN&GE Joint Railway agreeing,

54. The lonely branch
terminus at Fockerby
in June 1958.
D. Thompson

55. The Peat Moss rail system at Hatfield Moor survives, and was visited on 31 March 1974. *Author*

56. Commemorative medallion issued on the cutting of the first sod
of the Isle of Axholme Light Railway on 20 July 1899.
Collection G. Sellers. Photograph T. J. Lodge

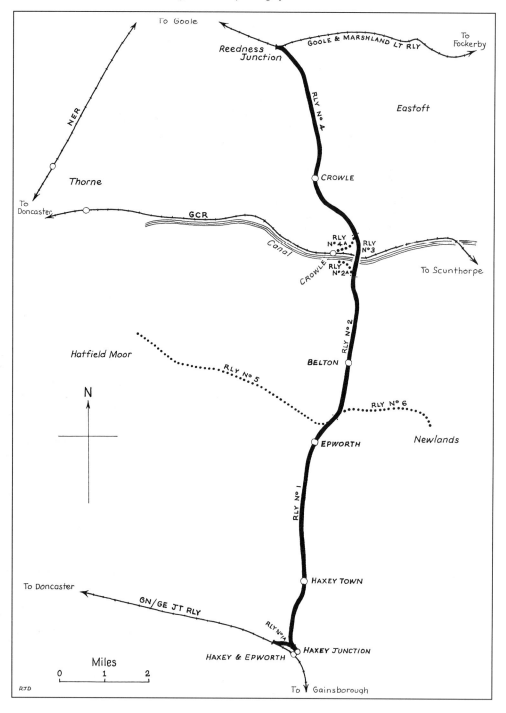

To Goole

GOOLE & MARSHLAND LT RLY

Reedness
Junction

To
Fockerby

Eastoft

RLY Nº 4

NER

Thorne

CROWLE

To
Doncaster

GCR

To Scunthorpe

Canal

RLY
Nº 4A

RLY
Nº 3

CROWLE

RLY
Nº 2A

RLY Nº 2

Hatfield Moor

RLY Nº 5

BELTON

RLY Nº 6

N

Newlands

EPWORTH

RLY Nº 1

HAXEY TOWN

To Doncaster

GN/GE JT RLY

RLY Nº 1A

HAXEY JUNCTION

HAXEY & EPWORTH

Miles

0   1   2

RJD

To Gainsborough

57 The Isle of Axholme Light Railway

70

58. Reedness Junction in May 1959 looking east, the line to Haxey on the right and to Fockerby on the left. Note as at most stations the high standard of maintenance in spite of the passenger service having been withdrawn in 1933. *D. Thompson*

provided there were protective clauses.

The Chairman, the Earl of Jersey, said the Commissioners had great pleasure in recommending that an Order be issued in this case. They were glad they had found little opposition to the scheme, only the desire of gentlemen present to give suggestions which would make the line better for the people. He congratulated the latter on having local gentlemen who had come forward with a local scheme for the benefit of the locality. He sincerely hoped the district would be better for it.

The Light Railway Order for lines as outlined above was approved by the Board of Trade on 11 March 1899. Contracts were let in May to White and Meyer, now engaged on the construction of the G&MLR. The 'first sod' was cut at Epworth on 17 July 1899, complete with procession and brass bands. The ceremony was performed by Miss Bletcher, the daughter of the Chairman of the Company, who was presented with a silver spade by Mr Meyer. This was followed by a 'free meat tea' for 1,500 people. The day ended with a fireworks display and a fire at a straw stack. The newspaper does not state whether the two events were connected.

By 1900 P.R. Meyer was one of the Directors. During that year Sebastian was asked what exactly was his position with the Company. He replied that he was a 'general factotum'. In June it was recorded that the Yorkshire District Light Railway

Syndicate held 4,267 shares to the value of £21,335 (the first reference to the connection between Sebastian's Syndicate and the Light Railway). Before the end of the year, although construction had only just started, the NER had decided to take over from the Company. The article from the *Doncaster Gazette*, already quoted, continued 'The Isle of Axholme will be a mineral line as well as an agricultural one and will carry most of the coal for South Carr Colliery. The ramifications are not to be confined to the Goole & Marshland and the Isle of Axholme. The NER have desired direct access to the Derbyshire Coalfields and they intend to ask Parliament to sanction the acquisition of powers already granted by the Light Railway Commissioners for a Light Railway from Haxey to Tickhill'. It was also stated that a large tonnage of iron ore from Frodingham for shipment at Goole would be put on the line for carriage via Crowle. The route would be 15 miles shorter than by Stainforth, but, as the connection at Crowle faced the wrong direction, this routing is not very clear.

In July 1901 the NER decided on the form of the swing-bridge at Crowle. It was to be modelled on the design of a bridge on the proposed North Holderness Light Railway over the River Hull at Groveshill. It was to be wide enough for double track, although only one line was put in.

An inspection of the line took place on 25 November 1901, when the first engine with a

59. Sentinel steam railcar at Crowle on a north bound working. Note the very low platforms, typical of the line. *G. J. Aston*

carriage conveying the Directors and their guests arrived at Epworth. It must have crossed the Stainforth & Keadby Canal on a temporary bridge as Oates in his *Axholme Joint Railway* (p.8) states that work on the swing bridge did not start until midway through 1902. This train was met by some 400 people; ceremonial shots were fired, and speeches made by Dunstan and Standring (the contractors) praising the men engaged on the works.

The NER Act of 1902 also authorised the purchase of the IOALR by the NER and the L&YR Companies, at a price of £27,500, reflecting the amount of work which had been done on the line. The 4 per cent Debenture stock was repaid at 102. The Axholme Joint Railway Committee was set up by the Act to administer the two lines.

Although the Meyers' direct connection with the line now ceased, some of its subsequent history is of interest. The Joint Committee opened the line from Reedness Junction to Fockerby and to Crowle for all traffic on 10 August 1903. The first train left Goole at 7.45 a.m, consisting of an L&Y

GOOLE, FOCKERBY, CROWLE, and HAXEY JUNCTION (One class only).—Lancashire and Yorkshire and North Eastern.
Sec., H. Marriott, Hunt's Bank, Manchester. Supt., M. Woodhouse, Crowle.

Miles	Down.	Week Days only.						
		mrn	mrn	mrn	aft	aft	aft	aft
			Sats. only.	Wednesdays only.	Except Wednesdays.	Sats. only.	Except Saturdays.	Saturdays only.
	Goole ....dep.	7 5	9 25	1150	1218	3 10	5 30	5 45
5¾	Reedness Junction ....arr.	7 17	9 37	12 2	1230	3 22	5 42	5 57
—	Reedness Junction ..dep.	....		12 6	1234		5 46	6 1
8¾	Eastoft........	....		1215	1243		5 55	6 10
10	Luddington	....		1219	1247		5 59	6 14
11¾	Fockerby ....arr.	....		1223	1251		6 3	6 18
—	Reedness Junction ....dep.	7 18	9 38	12 4	1232	3 23	5 44	5 59
8¾	Crowle 692, 698.... arr.	7 26	9 46	1212	1240	3 31	5 52	6 7
	Crowle 692, 698.... dep.	7 27	9 47	1213	1241	3 32	5 53	6 8
13	Belton........	7 39	9 59	1225	1253	3 44	6 5	6 20
14¾	Epworth	7 45	10 5	1231	1259	3 50	6 11	6 26
17¾	Haxey Town........	7 53	1013	1239	1 7	3 58	6 19	6 34
19½	Haxey Junction 359..arr.	7 57	1017	1243	1 11	4 2	6 23	6 38

Miles	Mls	Up.	Week Days only.									
			mrn	mrn	mrn	mrn	aft	aft	aft	aft	aft	aft
			Except Saturdays.		Sats. only.	Sats. only.	Weds. only.	Sats. only.	Except Wednesdays.	Sats. only.	Except Saturdays.	Sats. only.
		Haxey Junction ....dep.		8 6		1043	1257		1 30	4 20	6 36	6 51
1¾		Haxey Town........		8 11		1048	1 2		1 35	4 25	6 41	6 56
4¾		Epworth		8 20		1056	1 10		1 43	4 33	6 49	7 4
6½		Belton........		8 27		11 3	1 17		1 50	4 40	6 56	7 11
10¾		Crowle........ arr.		8 38		1114	1 28		2 1	4 51	7 7	7 22
		Crowle........ dep.		8 39		1115	1 29		2 2	4 52	7 8	7 23
13¾		Reedness Junction ......arr.		8 47		1123	1 37		2 10	5 0	7 16	7 31
—		Fockerby ....dep.	8 25	....	1024		1 17	1 48	....		6 9	6 23
—	1½	Luddington	8 29	....	1028		1 21	1 52	....		6 13	6 27
—	2¾	Eastoft........	8 33	....	1032		1 25	1 56	....		6 17	6 31
—	5¾	Reedness Junction ..arr.	8 42	....	1042		1 34	2 5	....		6 26	6 40
—		Reedness Junction ......dep.	....	8 52	1043	1124	1 42	....	2 12	5 1	7 17	7 32
19½		Goole 772 *and above*....arr.	....	9 5	1055	1136	1 55	....	2 24	5 13	7 29	7 45

60. Timetable for the Goole–Haxey Junction line from the May 1914 'Bradshaw'.

61. A freight working at Reedness Junction on the Fockerby line loop. Looking west. *Author*

locomotive and three carriages. The service was from Goole to Fockerby (or Crowle), returning to Reedness Junction and then proceeding to Crowle (or Fockerby) and then returning via Reedness to Goole. There were two trains in each direction on six days a week, with an additional train on Wednesday and Saturday. The three carriages were hired from the L&Y by the Committee.

The Contractors had been relieved of working the lines from Marshland to Crowle and Fockerby from 1 July 1903. In November of that year a Deed was executed between the Joint Committee and Sebastian Meyer for the construction of station buildings, station masters' houses and weigh offices at Haxey Junction, Haxey, Epworth and Belton at a total cost of £4,231 8s 5d to be completed in six months. The sub-contractors were Messrs James Bryant & Sons of York.

The Officers' Conference of 13 October 1904 reported that the connecting line at Haxey Junction 'was merely a contractor's junction'. The authorised junction had not been constructed and the powers for it had lapsed. The NER considered

that the line should be taken out, but the L&YR said it should remain. That this course prevailed is shown by the fact that the connection is included in the Railway Clearing House maps and junction diagrams of the district. It was decided that goods trains would start to run to Haxey Junction on 14 November 1904. It was hoped to commence the passenger service, but delay was caused by an accident to a crane at the swing-bridge which had to be operated by manual power for some time after that date.

Passenger services to Haxey Junction began on 2 January 1905. No connections were given with GN&GE trains. In fact no arrangements had been made with the Joint Line for the exchange of traffic. There were passenger stations at Crowle, Belton, Epworth, Haxey Town and Haxey Junction. One was planned at Burnham, between Epworth and Haxey, but was not proceeded with. There were passing places at Crowle, Belton (installed 1907), Epworth and Haxey Town. These were protected by home signals, and at first it was considered that distant signals were not necessary.

The use of an 'autocar' was investigated, but it was thought there would be no saving as 'ordinary trains' would be required on Wednesdays and Saturdays. The line had to wait until 1926 before it saw a rail-car, when a LNER Sentinel-Cammel steam coach was tried. In 1930 the Committee acquired its own Sentinel-Cammel coach, the only motive power it ever possessed. By this time, unfortunately, it was adequate for the Market Day traffic. It was taken over by the LNER in 1933 on the cessation of the passenger service.

Between 1904 and 1909 there are frequent references to consultations between Mr Bayley of the L&YR (acting for the Joint Committee) and Meyer as to the terms under which the siding from the British Moss Litter Works to the G&M line at Swinefleet was originally laid. Meyer stated that the Moss Litter Company had no permission from him to admit traffic other than their own. Meyer is referred to as one of the promoters of the G&M. A tramway from a peat works to Swinefleet crossed the G&M between Marshland and Reedness Junction, and although no indication has been found in the records as to which concern was attempting to cross or get access to the NER and L&Y systems, it may well have been in connection with the sinking of Thorne Colliery.

In 1905 the Joint Committee had obtained the Axholme Joint Railway (Hatfield Moor Extension)

Light Railway Order for a line from Epworth to the Peat Works on Hatfield Moor. The line was opened throughout on 1 March 1909 from a north facing junction at Epworth in place of the south facing one of the earlier order.

In June 1908, the L&YR jointly with the NER, applied to the Light Railway Commissioners for an Order for the Hatfield Moor Further Extension Railway, a line from Hatfield Moor to the Dearne Valley Railway at Black Carr, near Doncaster, in

63. Crowle (North) looking south.
Author

Alderman Sebastian Meyer of York, he was the first witness before the Select Committee of the House of Lords in March 1909. He stated there were no railways in the district and that the new line was intended to help agriculture. The officers of the L&YR and the NER present at the hearing must have smiled quietly at this. He went on to say that he had laid out the Goole & Marshland and the Isle of Axholme Light Railways, but they had not been planned as a through route, and that he had designed the Dearne Valley Railway. The Extension would be of assistance to the DVR as it would provide an eastern outlet for DVR traffic. But it was not intended to provide passenger facilities.

Evidence in support was given by local farmers. D. C. Rattray, the Engineer of the L&YR, said that there would be two stations. But, in view of Meyer's statement, these would probably have been goods stations. One of these, by agreement with Lord Fitzwilliam, would have been near Armthorpe. The Earl would have had the right to require the building of a branch railway, about two miles long, to serve the proposed colliery (which later became Markham Main).

Lord Allerton, Chairman of the GNR (among others) opposed the Bill as he owned a large coal-bearing estate on Hatfield Moor and the new line would prevent access to the Stainforth & Keadby Canal and to the GCR for the carriage of coal

connection with proposed development in the district. It was strongly opposed by the Great Central Railway, so the Commissioners had no alternative but to refuse the application immediately.

The two Companies then applied to Parliament in November 1908 with a Bill for the Hatfield Moor Further Extension Light Railway. Meyer's last appearance in connection with the Axholme railways was in 1909, when, given his full title of

62. *above:* The swing bridge and viaduct at Crowle across the ex-Great Central line from Doncaster to Scunthorpe and the Stainforth & Keadby canal (over which is the opening span). Looking west. *Author*

64. Crowle (North) looking north in June 1958. Note the station house with wooden office on the right. *D. Thompson*

65. Belton station looking north in June 1958. Note the substantial station house. *D. Thompson*

from his proposed mine.

After arrangements had been made with Lord Allerton, the Bill was passed on 16 August 1909. It is obvious that, had the line been constructed it would have provided a much shorter alternative route for South Yorkshire coal traffic to an East Coast port than the one denied to Meyer on the curtailment of his Tickhill proposal (Chapter 9). The railway was not built, but the L&YR, the NER and their successors considered it of sufficient importance for their powers to be renewed until they finally lapsed in 1932.

66. Epworth station looking north in June 1958. *D. Thompson*

67. The Sentinel railcar at Haxey Junction. 'Axholme Joint Railway' appears in full on the sides of the saloon. The IOAJt platform was at some distance from those of the GN&GE Joint line. *G. J. Aston*

On the Goole & Marshland Light Railway there were few engineering features, the only one being the 120 foot long bridge across the Swinefleet Warping Drain. Much of the line has reverted to agriculture and today is untraceable. The station houses at Reedness Junction and at Luddington stand in splendid isolation. The Isle of Axholme Light Railway, as constructed by the NE and L&YR, presented a very different picture. About 1½ miles from Crowle (North) Station the line rose on an embankment to cross the Stainforth & Keadby Canal (Sheffield and South Yorkshire Navigation). The viaduct and swing-bridge were the largest engineering structure on the railway. It commenced with three brick arches, which crossed a minor road and a drain, followed by a girder bridge over the Doncaster to Scunthorpe branch of the GCR. Another brick arch was crossed before the swing-bridge. This was of 'hog-backed' lattice-girder construction, 108 feet long. The pier was situated on the south bank of the Navigation and

the bridge was swung by means of a Crossley oil engine. The bridge was built by the Cleveland Bridge & Engineering Company at a cost of £20,000. As the original estimate of White for its construction was £6,200, it is interesting to speculate on the form he intended. The structure ended in another brick arch.

Half a mile south of the swing-bridge, the Doncaster to Scunthorpe road, the Double Rivers and the River Thorne were crossed on a twelve-arch viaduct. Soon after this a similar nine-arch viaduct spanned the New River Idle and other drainage channels. After Belton Station the line ran on an embankment and crossed the Goole to Gains-borough road on an underline bridge. All this has been swept away and the site turned into a pleasant picnic area. The line next entered a cutting. But before this the Hatfield Moor branch came in from the west and the line through the cutting had the appearance of a double track, the actual junction being at Epworth Station. This cutting has now

68. Haxey Town station (looking north), June 1958. *D. Thompson*

been largely filled in. The station was built on an embankment and the station master's house was some distance away at ground level.

A road was bridged and a substantial embankment followed. But at Haxey Town the line was again in cutting, which is now a nature reserve with a footpath. Haxey Junction was approached on an embankment. The Deposited Plans show two level crossings at Epworth and two at Haxey. But at three of these sites bridges were built showing the importance which the two companies placed on their new acquisition. The stations too were better built and appointed than was usual on light railways, but the platforms were low. All the station masters' houses are still in use as private residences.

The lines were all single. Marshland Junction to

Reedness Junction was worked by electric train staff and Reedness to Haxey Junction by electric tablet. Reedness Junction to Fockerby and Epworth to Hatfield Moor were both worked by 'one engine in steam'.

Passenger services were withdrawn from the Axholme Joint Railway on 17 July 1933. Haxey Junction to Epworth was closed to all traffic on 1 February 1956, but the rails were not lifted until 1962. The Hatfield Moor branch finished on 30 September 1963 and the remainder closed on 5 April 1965. The section from Belton to Marshland Junction was transferred to the Central Electricity Generating Board and maintained in the hope of the construction of a power station at Belton. But this did not materialise and the line was lifted and the swing bridge demolished in 1972.

CHAPTER NINE

The Tickhill Light Railway

THE Tickhill Light Railway was proposed in 1899, the promoters named in the Order being William McDonnel Mackay, G. H. Newborn and C. D. Nicholson. The first was an analytical chemist and was later associated with Meyer in the Oleine factory. He was a Director of the IOALR. Newborn was a partner in the firm of solicitors of Epworth who acted for the Company, and the last was a local farmer and landowner and also a Director of the IOALR. Plans were deposited for a line from the Dearne Valley Railway at St Catherine's to Tickhill on much the same course as the A1(M) of today, then on to Bawtry, with west- and east-facing connections to the Great Northern main line, and through Misson to end at the south side of Haxey station on the GN&GE Joint line, with a connection which was to cross the Joint line on a girder bridge to a junction with the IOALR. Its length was about seventeen miles and it was said that 'it would complete a network of feeders to the main lines in south-east Yorkshire and north-west Lincolnshire. The connection with the DVR will give the mining district an alternative route for export.' Mr L. B. Wells was the Engineer and the estimated cost was £87,541.

The Public Inquiry before the Light Railway Commissioners, the Earl of Jersey and Colonel Boughey, into the proposals was held in the Guild Hall, Doncaster, on 1 June 1900. Counsel for the promoters said the railway would aid the agricultural needs of the district and would also form a mineral line. Meyer was the first witness. He said he was Secretary of the DVR and was connected with the Goole & Marshland and the Isle of Axholme Railways. 'He had taken part in light railways and had promoted large numbers of them'. He was one of the promoters of the scheme and was also connected with the proposed South Carr Colliery which the new line would serve.

Early in the proceedings, Railway No.1, just over four miles long from the DVR to Tickhill, was withdrawn from the application on the objection of the Right Hon. J. G. Savile-Foljambe, a landowner at Wadworth. J. J. Addy, Chairman of the DVR and Managing Director of Carlton Main and Grimethorpe Collieries, expressed disappointment, but it was hoped that a route on a better alignment could be agreed later.

Considerable opposition was received from the GNR and from the GN&GE Joint Committee. Their Counsel stated that they had not objected to the DVR and to the IOALR which they regarded as feeders and they had 'displayed enlightened self-interest' with regard to the junctions with these lines, but this was 'an insidious through route'.

The Commissioners were not convinced as sufficient evidence of competition had not been shown to justify refusing approval. The question was left to the final decision of the Board of Trade.

There were persistent reports in such diverse papers as the *Colliery Guardian* and the *Goole Times* that the North Eastern Railway, which had hastily withdrawn from Parliament its proposals for a similar line, would apply in the next Session to take over the powers to be granted to the Light Railway, but no proof of this has been found. Nottingham County Council feared that, if the line were built by the NER, that company would not provide as good facilities to the local public.

In February 1901 Newborn and Meyer as pro-

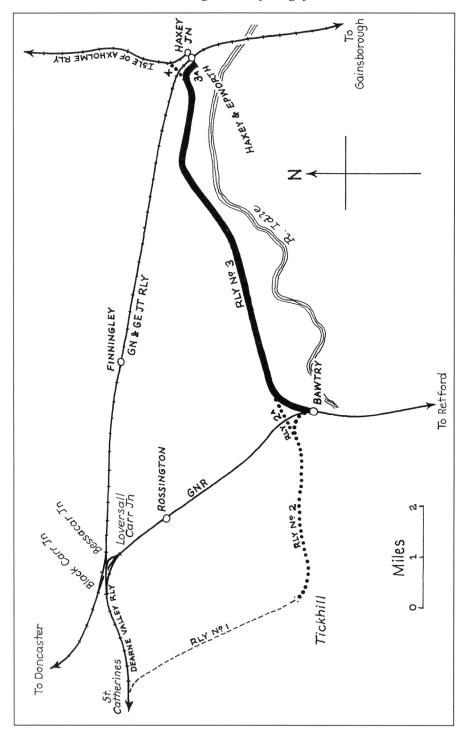

69. The Tickhill Light Railway.

moters and Wells as Engineer, with representatives of the proposed Rotherham, Tinsley & Tickhill Light Railway (there were repeated rumours of the sinking of a mine at Tickhill at this time, and a junction between the two Light Railways could easily have been effected), appeared before Sir Courtenay Boyle, President of the Board of Trade. Their arguments must have been successful as the Light Railway Order for a line from Tickhill to Bawtry and Haxey was granted on 7 August 1901.

Nothing was done in the way of building and it was necessary to re-apply to the Commissioners for an Extension of Time for the completion of the railway. The Light Railway Order of 22 September 1904 granted this for a further three years.

By 1907 there had been no raising of money, land purchase or line construction. It was now stated that the sinking of a colliery at Tickhill was 'impossible'. The capital of the Company had been fixed at £81,000, with borrowing powers of £27,000. About 2,300 shares had been taken up by or were allotted to the promoters themselves but they were unable to raise any further capital. In fact, no shares were issued to the public. The promoters, therefore, approached the L&YR and the NER jointly together with the GNR with a view to a takeover.

The joint companies, in spite of the newspaper stories of a few years earlier, were not interested; they had access to the district by the South Yorkshire Joint line. The GNR, which could not afford the possibility of the line falling into other hands, decided it would be in its interest to take over the Light Railway. An Inquiry was held in Doncaster on 6 July 1907. There was some opposition from the L&YR and NER Railways, who feared a lower rate for the carriage of coal via Doncaster than via the IOALR, but this question was resolved. The GNR agreed to construct the line from Tickhill to Haxey, with exchange sidings at the latter. However it stated it would not make a junction with the South Yorkshire line at Tickhill, to the annoyance of the Great Central Railway which stated it had been promised running powers to Bawtry.

The Light Railway Order of 4 November 1908 authorised the transfer of the Light Railway to the GNR and granted yet another Extension of Time for four more years. The *Yorkshire Post* stated that 'the purchase may not be unconnected with the proposed developments on Hatfield Moor'.

Meyer, of course, now had no further interest in the railway, so it is only necessary to give a brief outline of its subsequent history. In the following year it was reported that the railway was about to be started, but that the GNR was waiting for coal-sinking to be commenced. It was said that the coal might go to Boston. Early in 1910 contracts were advertised and, by July, notices to treat were served on the landowners for the purchase of the land for the whole length of the railway. It was decided that Railway No.4, the junction line to the IOALR, could be dispensed with, in spite of assurances that it would be built. The contract for a single line some eight miles long from Bawtry to Haxey, to be constructed in twelve months, was awarded to Messrs Henry Lovatt & Co. at a price of £30,000.

Work started early in 1911 and progress was rapid. The line was opened from Bawtry to Haxey on 26 August 1912 for mineral traffic but it is very doubtful if it was ever used as a through route. There were sand and gravel pits near Bawtry and agricultural produce could be picked up along the line. Although the branches to Tickhill and to the IOALR were not built, the GNR thought it worthwhile to keep the powers for them alive until 1925. By 1930 conditions had altered and a small area of land near Tickhill, purchased in 1912, from Lord Scarbrough for £10, was sold back to him for £5 by the LNER. Other landowners, many with a much greater acreage, were dealt with in a similar fashion. As there was inflation, even in those days, the railway had to make the best of a bad bargain.

As this part of the country is comparatively flat, little engineering was called for in the building of the Tickhill Light Railway. But, like the Axholme Joint line, the GNR constructed the branch to 'heavy' standards and there was a girder bridge, approached by an embankment, over an unclassified road near Haxey. Other minor roads were only protected by cattle guards. A short section was in cutting which, at times, resembles a canal rather than a railway but, like the Goole & Marshland, much of the course has reverted to agriculture.

The line was worked by 'one engine in steam', with Train Staff and Annett's Key. The speed limit was 25 m.p.h., but only ten over level crossings.

After an uneventful existence, the line finally closed to all traffic on 1 April 1965, although for many years it had been used for storing surplus wagons.

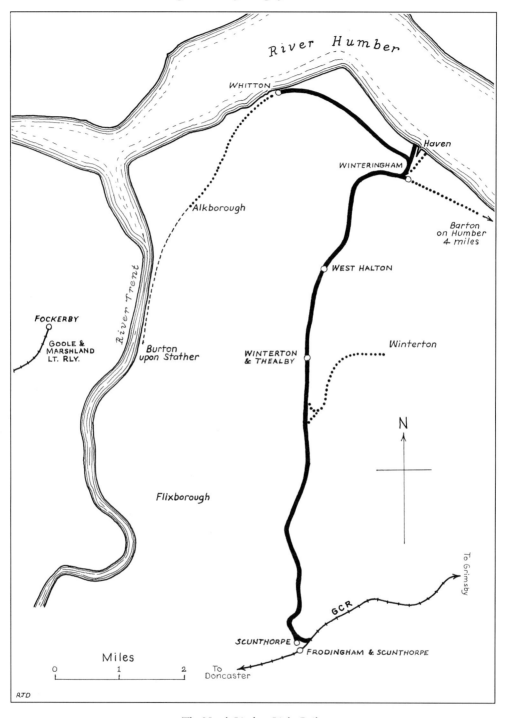

70. The North Lindsey Light Railway.

CHAPTER TEN

The North Lindsey Light Railways and the Leeds Contract Company

THE story of the relationship between the North Lindsey Light Railways Company, the Leeds Contract Company and the Great Central Railway Company is a complicated one and may be compared to a three-handed game of poker, with the cards held very firmly to the chest by the players. At a later date it was made more involved by the intervention of a fourth player, the Lancashire & Yorkshire Company. Narration is not helped by the fact that the first two contestants were practically the same people but, while the records of the Light Railway are full, few of those of the Contract Company have been found by the author.

A Light Railway was proposed in May 1896 from the Manchester, Sheffield & Lincolnshire Railway at Scunthorpe, through Normanby, Thealby, Colsby and West Halton to Winteringham and, through Winterton, back to the MS&LR near Appleby. A committee was set up in Scunthorpe to consider this.

The North Lindsey Light Railways Company was promoted by Major William George Dove, R. Goodworth and W. Glazier. Plans were prepared in April 1898 and a Public Inquiry before the Light Railway Commissioners took place at the Station Hotel, Frodingham on 23 September 1898. The Engineer of the scheme was Lionel B. Wells of Manchester and the Solicitors Milling & Dodgson of Rothwell, Leeds. The main line was to run from the centre of Frodingham to Winteringham Haven. A branch was proposed from the GCR (which the MS&LR had become) near North Lincoln signal box to the main line beyond Normanby Park, and others from Roxby to Winterton, from near West

Halton to Alkborough and from Winteringham to Whitton. The estimated cost was just over £70,000.

Counsel for the promoters said a similar scheme had been talked about for at least fifteen years. Lord Carrington's representative stated that the people of the district were strongly in favour and that the line would greatly benefit agriculture. Mr Wells declared there was no difficulty in building the line and where it crossed the ironstone beds compensation would be paid. Questioned by Mr F. Parker Rhodes, Solicitor to the Midland Ironstone Company and a well known legal expert on railway matters, he admitted that he had not correctly estimated the amount of compensation which would have to be paid out. Unusually, the Commissioners postponed giving their decision.

A month later they announced that the scheme required further consideration and needed important amendments before it could be approved. The application therefore failed and the project remained in abeyance. Widespread disappointment was expressed in the district and the local paper hoped the promoters would not lose heart.

Indeed they did not and a modified plan was deposited within a few weeks. The main line would now run more to the south and east of the ironstone area near Frodingham and terminate at Whitton. Winteringham Haven and Winterton were both to be served by branches. The estimated cost had risen to just over £80,000.

The second inquiry was held at the Scunthorpe Assembly Rooms on 16 February 1899. An alternative was agreed with Lord Carrington that the main line would pass through Winteringham. There was no serious opposition and the Commissioners stated they would be glad to recommend the Board of Trade to sanction the scheme.

The Leeds Contract Company was formed that year to finance the Light Railway. The original shareholders were Edward Sisterson, Sebastian Meyer, James W. Close and George Dove, each holding 251 shares, with Messrs Robson, Walls and Walker holding a nominal one share each. The first four shareholders were Directors of the Company, but Meyer resigned in 1903. The capital was £10,000.

The Light Railway Order was approved by the Board of Trade on 29 January 1900, on which date the North Lindsey Light Railways Company was incorporated. The promoters were now given as William Inglis, Major George Dove, Horace Milling and Walter Dodgson.

The railway near Frodingham and near Winteringham was not to be built without the consent of Lord St Oswald. Rowland Winn, second Baron St Oswald of Nostell Priory near Ackworth and of Appleby (Lincs), was one of the largest land owners in the district and well aware of the valuable deposits of ironstone on his estates. His father, also Rowland, was one of the founders of the Trent, Ancholme & Grimsby Railway of 1861, which put Frodingham on the railway map. He became first Baron in 1885.

An Amendment Order was applied for in 1901, with an inquiry at Frodingham in February 1902, to allow an alteration to the junction with the GCR, now to be made to the east of Frodingham station. (This was the original junction about a mile east of the present Scunthorpe station). The application was approved and submitted to the Board of Trade on 17 December 1904, but it was allowed to stand over, pending negotiations between the promoters and the landowners.

At the end of 1901 Walter Dodgson reported that he had been unable to get the consent of one landowner in reasonable terms and that no work had been done. He was considering applying to the Commissioners for Compulsory Powers.

After these difficulties had been resolved the 'first sod' was cut at Thealby in 'wretched weather' on 7 January 1901. After the usual cold luncheon, including 'a liberal supply of champagne', Major Dove presented Sir Berkeley Sheffield with a silver spade with which he 'turned the first sod in a workmanlike manner'. Among those present were

Sebastian Meyer and Z. G. Yewdall, Chief Draughtsman, of Frodingham.

At the end of the year an important and far-reaching Agreement was made with the GCR – that the Company would work the Light Railway for 60 per cent of the gross receipts.

The NLLR's Amendment Order was at last settled and approved by the Board of Trade on 30 January 1905. Railway No.1a, from the sidings of the GCR at Frodingham to a junction with the line authorised in 1900, had to be agreed with Lord St Oswald. But this had already been arranged. It was agreed with the Midland Ironstone Co. (a combine of the Staveley Coal & Iron Co., John Brown & Co. and Parkgate Iron & Steel Co.) that the Company could consign its own traffic to Frodingham at a through rate fixed at ½d per ton. The Ironstone Co. was to marshall the trains and provide engine power, wagons and labour. A similar arrangement continues to the present time – locomotives of the Midland Ironstone Co., Frodingham Iron & Steel Co., United Steel, and British Steel Corporation having in turn enjoyed running powers.

Early in the year the tender from the Leeds Contract Co. to build the line for £84,185 was accepted. The Company was allotted 1,200 £10 shares and in July it received 500 further shares.

About this time William Inglis, one of the first Directors, died. Sebastian and Philip Robert Meyer were made Directors and the latter appointed Secretary at a salary of £100 per annum. The Directors were to be paid £100 per annum. Sebastian Meyer was also to be paid £300 per annum 'for his special service as Engineer' from 1 December 1904. He was paid a further £500 'for services rendered during the four years ending 1903'. The offices of the Company were now at 13 Bond Street, Leeds.

No sooner had construction of the line begun than the Directors started to think of expansion. In May 1905 plans were deposited for an extension from Winteringham to the sidings of the GCR at Barton-on-Humber and from Whitton to Burton-upon-Stather, a total of some 11½ miles, at an estimated cost of £80,582 10s. F. S. Wheat was the Engineer. These extensions were initiated by the GCR, which was prepared to work them.

The public inquiry was held at Barton on 5 July. Only four months earlier the Commissioners had

71. The first passenger train from Winterton to Scunthorpe, 3 September 1906.
Humberside Libraries

held an inquiry in the same town on the Ackworth & Lindsey Light Railway which would have tunnelled under the Trent and run along the south bank of the Humber to Immingham. This had been immediately turned down by the Commissioners. There were now two rival schemes to be considered. The first was the Barton Light Railway, a curtailed version of the A&LLR prepared by the promoters of that line, and the second, the NLLR scheme. The Barton Light Railway's promoters were persuaded to withdraw, leaving the field clear for the NLLR.

The line to Barton had no serious opposition. The section between Alkborough and Burton-upon-Stather, said to be for the benefit of agriculture and to open up a pretty and attractive district to tourist traffic, was strongly objected to by Sir Berkeley Sheffield and Mr Constable, both of whom had been greatly in favour of the original aims of the Company. Sir Berkeley said the line would go through and spoil 1½ miles of his best shooting. Mr Constable said it was unnecessary to open up a quiet and secluded area with little hope of adequate financial return. He later wrote to the

Commissioners that the line was only a blocking measure to prevent any other railway company crossing the Trent and would not have been put forward by the NLLR had it not been for the A&LLR proposals. The Commissioners approved the line to Barton, but curtailed the branch from Whitton at Alkborough.

During the year Mrs Emily Meyer (Mrs P.R. Meyer) took up 250 Debenture shares. In November Edward Sisterson offered 300 tons of 'slightly defective' rails, but it was decided they were not required. He was, however, paid £7,000 for materials supplied, which he accepted in Lloyds Bonds.

At the end of the year Philip Meyer, as Secretary of the NLLR, wrote to D.S. Hartmann, Secretary to the Leeds Contract Co. (at the same address) that the Midland Ironstone Co. had a right of way over the Light Railway from their mines at Crosby Warren to Frodingham on payment of a nominal toll of ½d per ton from the beginning of 1907. The Contract Co. had to maintain the line during the period of the contract and to provide the signalling. Meyer therefore proposed that the Contract Co. should have the ½d per ton. He continued 'with regard to your application to carry agricultural traffic during the construction of the railway, there is no objection to your doing so at rates to be agreed between the parties interested, and at your own risk'.

Sir Berkeley Sheffield was elected to the Board in December 1905, in spite of his opposition to the extension to Burton-on-Stather. He became a Director of the GCR in 1909, holding both offices until the 1923 Grouping.

The period 1906–7 was one of great activity in the field of railway politics in North Lincolnshire. Early in 1906 both the NLLR and L&YR purchased land near Winteringham Haven. In May Roland Burke, agent to Sir Berkeley Sheffield, was elected a Director of the NLLR.

About this time the first shots in the battle were heard, as witnessed in the following L&YR minute of 25 April 1906:

Mr Aspinall [General Manager] and Sir George Armitage [Chairman] reported that, when in London,

they had a call from the Directors of the NLLR who, notwithstanding they were under certain obligations to the GCR Co. and had entered Agreements with that Company, they were anxious to open negotiations with the L&Y Co. with a view to their scheme being taken over by the L&YR. Mr Aspinall explained that the powers of the NLLR Co.'s Order entitled that Company to make a line from Frodingham to Winteringham, from Winteringham to Barton and from Whitton to Alkborough. [He was a little previous in this, as the Order had not yet been confirmed.]

He explained the advantages to the L&YR in taking over the line and pointed out that the NLLR would, in the event of arrangements being made, apply for powers to cross the Trent to Fockerby. It was pointed out that the line would serve that part of Lincolnshire where the Frodingham iron ore was raised in very large quantities and, in a very short time, large industries would spring up along the line.

The difficulty Mr Aspinall had in entertaining any proposal from the NLLR was in the fact that they appeared to have some Agreement with the GCR Co., but the Directors of the NLLR considered they would be

72. A peaceful scene at Winteringham Haven looking across the Humber estuary in 1987. It might have rivalled Immingham. *Author*

able to get out of the Agreements with the GCR and, of course, if they could do this, it would be to the advantage of the L&YR to enter into negotiations with them.

It was resolved that, provided the NLLR can obtain cancellation of the Agreements they have entered into with the GCR Co., Mr Aspinall was to be authorised to inform them that the L&YR Co. were willing to enter into an arrangement with them if suitable terms can be agreed.

The North Lindsey Light Railways Extension Order was confirmed on 10 July 1906 for the branches to Barton and to Alkborough, although the Commissioners had recommended an end-on junction at Barton and the diversion of a road to avoid the necessity of two level crossings. The Company received powers to raise a further £75,000, which could include the issue of £25,000 Preference shares.

The Light Railway was opened to goods and passenger traffic from Scunthorpe to Winterton & Thealby on Monday 3 September, the first train leaving the Company's own station at Dawes Lane, Scunthorpe at 7.35 am. There were three trains a day in each direction.

In September the L&Y Board again minuted:

The Chairman and the General Manager had seen the promoters of the NLLR and they had been unable to come to any satisfactory agreement with regard to the L&YR purchasing or obtaining Running Powers from Alkborough to Winteringham and from Winteringham to Scunthorpe. The General Manager had seen Mr Simpson, Solicitor to the Light Railway. The most satisfactory arrangement would be for the L&Y Co. to buy up the powers of the North Lindsey from Alkborough to Winteringham if it can be done on reasonable terms. On the other hand, if they cannot come to terms with the Light Railway, it might be thought desirable to deposit a Bill next Session to construct from Fockerby to Alkborough and from that point, parallel with the Light Railway to Winteringham to the property they have already there for their steamboat traffic and also to obtain the traffic from the ironstone district. The North Eastern Railway is to be invited to join in.

It was ordered that, in view of the probable failure of negotiations with the NLLR Co., arrangements be made to deposit a Bill.

Mr Simpson later phoned to say that his clients would not consider the question of selling their powers as between Winteringham and Alkborough but they thought an independent company should construct a

line between Fockerby and Alkborough and then his clients would give Running Powers or would consider sale to the Company outright. The Chairman and the General Manager would be prepared to meet him and his clients when they had some definite proposals.

The projects were opposed by the NER, which is hardly surprising.

In October Sebastian Meyer reported that he had inspected the Haven at Winteringham and was very impressed by its capabilities, provided about £10,000 was spent on piling. Instructions were given to the Engineer to proceed with this as soon as possible. An application was received early in November from the L&YR to make a junction with the Light Railway at Winteringham. The Directors decided they must see the plan.

On 8 November Dixon H. Davies, Solicitor to the GCR, sent a written report to his Board which is so important that, even at the expense of some repetition, it is reproduced in full:

It has recently transpired that the L&YR Co. are surveying a line of railway to connect their system with the foreshore of the Humber at Winteringham where there is every reason to believe they have completed the purchase of some 300 acres from Lord Carrington. It will be remembered that about 1900, the L&Y and NER Cos. acquired the Goole & Marshland Light Railway which has been authorised for the development of the potato district lying to the west of the River Trent by connecting with the NER at Goole. This Light Railway ends at the village of Fockerby on the west bank of the Trent, six or seven miles from Winteringham. This acquisition could only be regarded as a menace to the Company's position in the Frodingham district and to meet it certain steps of a defensive nature were taken by us which it will be well to recall the Directors' recollection.

In 1900, Major Dove and Sir Berkeley Sheffield and some other gentlemen interested in the ironstone fields projected a railway called the North Lindsey Light Railways extending from a junction with the GCR at Frodingham to Winteringham, with a spur to Whitton Pier on the Trent *(sic)*. We entered into negotiations with these gentlemen and gave them a favourable Agreement for working the line. With the aid of this Agreement the Light Railway Company raised its capital and constructed their railway to West Halton, six miles, and is open to the public and has already resulted in a remarkable development of their ironstone field along it. The remainder of the work is in hand.

In the Session of 1904, the L&YR were in Parliament

with a scheme for running steamers and they included in a Bill general powers to purchase land and make quays anywhere on the Humber. The GCR succeeded in confining the services to Goole and Hull and limiting the acquisition of quays.

In November 1904, a proposal was deposited for a Light Railway from Ackworth to Immingham tunnelling the Trent between Fockerby and Whitton and following the coast through to Barton. This railway formed a junction with the Goole & Marshland Light Railway and evidently threatened an invasion by the L&YR and other Companies of the GCR's Lincolnshire district and the Immingham Dock. We strongly opposed it and it was defeated. Parts of it, including the Barton end, were re-deposited the following year by the same promoters. We not only opposed this but, with a view to countering the proposal, we asked the North Lindsey to deposit a scheme for this extension of their system to the GC line at Barton.

The independent scheme was withdrawn under pressure and the North Lindsey extension was passed. This extension included a spur to Burton-on-Stather, a point where it was supposed the tunnel under the Trent would emerge. Owing to a landowner's opposition, a couple of miles was cut off the end of this line which, as authorised, finishes at Alkborough. Following this the GCR entered an Agreement with the North Lindsey for the transfer of the powers for the extension. This Agreement, as also the Working Agreement, should receive Parliamentary sanction. The Company had no Bill in Parliament last year but, in view of the new move

of the L&YR, the Company should carefully consider whether the necessary authority can, with safety, be further postponed. Nothing in the way of opposition can be done to the L&Y proposal until we have the opportunity of seeing the actual scheme of the L&YR as deposited but the question is, are there any measures which could strengthen our position and to prejudice the promotion.

There is no doubt whatever that the North Lindsey people have been coquetting with the L&Y and, after consultation with the Chairman, I had an interview with the Chairman of the North Lindsey Company and asked him to explain what his Company's attitude towards the proposal was. He seemed to be anxious to evade the inquiry and stated it was a matter for his Board. I attended his Board yesterday (7 November) and requested them to approve the Working Agreement and also for the transfer of the extension. This approval, after some demur, they assented to, but stated that, as Sir Berkeley Sheffield, one of their most influential Directors, was not at the Board that day, they would like to adjourn the meeting until Tuesday next when the resolution would be passed. Meantime, they asked that the completion of the railway to Barton will be proceeded with. This, I think, the Directors will be well advised to assent to.

They asked for some support in the raising of further capital. The capital powers from the first Order are £60,000 Ordinary, £30,000 Preference and £30,000 Debentures. The Ordinary shares have been subscribed amongst landowners and promoters, the Debentures

73. Winteringham station in domestic use in 1987. *Author*

have all been arranged for and £6,000 of Preference have been taken up. I was asked if the Company would take up the remaining £24,000 Preference shares. It would not be worth the Company's while to take a financial interest in the concern unless they could get hold of it.

The third proposal of the North Lindsey Board was that the Company should assist in constructing a pier at Winteringham Haven. They had plans for this at a cost of £10,000 for a jetty which would enable vessels drawing thirteen feet of water to lie afloat at the end of the pier at the lowest spring tides, while a depth of sixteen feet six inches at low water would be reached by extending the pier another ten feet. This estimate does not cover the cost of the land, or the short railway to connect it. The land is an important factor in the general situation. Some of the Directors of the North Lindsey acquired some little time ago the whole of the present Winteringham Haven right down to the Humber shore, an area of about fourteen acres of land, including the franchise of the Lord of the Manor for the quay. I asked for an estimate and was told £15,000. Of course, I said such a figure was out of the question and it was arranged that Mr Meyer, one of the Directors and Manager, should come and see Mr Fay on Saturday next. If this land could be bought at a reasonable price (which would less than half the price asked) and if it can be connected to the Light Railway, it would seem desirable that the Company should take it up and the Bill might include powers for the purchase and for the connection. If the steps above recommended are to be carried through, the Company's answer to the L&YR's attack will be that they have continuously provided for every reasonable requirement of the district and are continuing to do so, and it will not be right to allow another Company to come out of its district and deprive us of the profits to which we legitimately looked forward when we undertook these interests. The danger of having the L&Y there at all is, not so much the shipping, as the important ironstone traffic at the Frodingham district, a large proportion of which would inevitably be diverted if such a railway were introduced.

It was resolved that the Company would submit a Bill for its protection.

These behind the scenes activities resulted in the deposition in November 1906 of a number a competing schemes. The most ambitious of these was that of the L&YR for a line from the termination of the former Goole & Marshland Light Railway at Fockerby, crossing the Trent by a bridge of six arches and two swinging spans near Trent Falls, through Alkborough and Whitton. It

then divided, one branch ending on the west side of Winteringham Haven and the other joining the North Lindsey, also near the west side of the Haven. The NLLR and the GCR both deposited plans for lines on either side of the Haven with powers to construct a pier or jetty into the Humber. The first was an application to the Light Railway Commissioners for an Order, the second was to Parliament for a Bill.

At the North Lindsey Board meeting on 13 November Major Dove, the Chairman, and Sebastian Meyer, having stated their interest in Winteringham Haven, said that the other owners, that is the Leeds Contract Co., were willing to sell the land to the Company at a price of £10,000. This was agreed to. Neither Dove nor Meyer voted.

Early in the new year, 1907, Davies reported to the GCR Board that the L&Y had submitted a Bill for a railway from Fockerby to Winteringham with power to construct a quay there and to run vessels. He said that there was no doubt that the Bill was the outcome of difficulties due to the silting up and shifting of the channel to Goole. He continued that the L&Y had an option or had acquired 300 acres of land at Winteringham around the Haven. The L&Y asked for running powers over the whole of the North Lindsey and powers to subscribe to it. He informed his Directors that the manorial rights in the Haven itself and some fourteen acres of land had recently been sold by Lord Carrington to certain Directors of the NLLR. 'As the land and the Haven are included within the limits of land to be acquired both by the L&YR Co and this Company, the ownership of this position becomes one of great strategic importance. It is a dangerous innovation for a line, which was acquiesced in and sanctioned as a Light Railway in a purely agricultural district, to be converted into a predatory attack upon another Company's district. The struggle will be a keen one'.

To counter this an Agreement was drafted between the GCR and the NLLR that the former would work the whole of the Light Railway and subscribe £125,000 towards it, which would enable the GCR to control the Company. The Agreement was a timely one for the Light Railway Company as at is recorded that the company owed £14,000 to the Leeds Contract Co, 'which they are unable to pay'. The contractors accepted £24,000 in 5 per cent Lloyds Bonds. In March pile-driving began at Winteringham on the Haven-side, Leggott & Speigh of Hull being the contractors.

In April, in the face of all-round opposition, the L&YR withdrew that part of its Bill relating to North Lincolnshire. In return the heads of an Agreement were settled between that Company and the GCR. The GCR was not to encroach on the property of the L&YR at Winteringham which it was to retain, but the GCR or the NLLR were to be allowed to have sufficient sea frontage to berth steamers up to 500 feet long. The GCR was not to object to the L&YR constructing a pier. The GCR was to agree to siding connections on both sides of the Haven but the L&YR was not to construct lines in competition with the NLLR. The GCR was to work the traffic which was to be exchanged at Doncaster or Askern. There were clauses with regard to territorial expansion by both companies in Lancashire and in Lincolnshire. This Agreement, however, was never formally ratified, as Davies, the GCR solicitor, feared he was giving too much away in Lincolnshire, but the L&YR Co. 'played ball' and it never again threatened to invade that part of Lincolnshire.

Following the Agreement between the GCR and the NLLR Companies, the former stated that it wished to have a majority in the number of Directors on the North Lindsey Board. That Company did not agree and it was decided that an Arbitrator be appointed. The line to Winteringham was officially opened on 15 July 1907, but a special excursion left Scunthorpe at 3.15 pm on Saturday 13 July carrying 234 people to the sports at Winteringham Feast. It returned at 10.30 pm. The regular service consisted of three trains a day, at a fare of 5d single and 10d return.

To begin with the arrangements were primitive: 'At Winteringham, there is no safe nor cash drawer. In fact, on the passenger platform there is no building. The only office is a small hut in the goods yard occupied by the porter-signalman. In this, there is a small desk with lift-up top which locks and this is the only place where cash can be secured. People who intend to travel will, to obtain their tickets, have to go inside this hut as there is no booking window, then retrace their steps out of the goods yard, over the level crossing, and on to the passenger platform but, if close on train time, the gates would be open, closing the crossing when people would naturally cross the line'.

The North Lindsey's proposals at Winteringham Harbour before the Light Railway Commissioners was withdrawn. The Great Central Bill, as far as the railway clauses were concerned, received no serious opposition. But the construction of the pier was opposed by the Board of Trade and other bodies. Wharves on the Humber and in Winteringham Haven were substituted. The Act was passed on 26 July 1907. It allowed the GCR to subscribe up to £130,000 to the Light Railway and to appoint three Directors. It confirmed the Agreement between the two Companies. The GCR was to work the Light Railway for 60 per cent of the gross receipts. Any surplus profits, after the Light Railway had paid dividends on the 5 per cent Preference shares and 4 per cent on the Ordinary shares, were to be divided equally between the two Companies. The Light Railway was not to sell or lease to any other railway. The powers were extended for a further two years. The GCR nominated Edward H. Fraser, R. N. Sutton Nelthorpe and Benjamin (*sic*) Day as Directors.

Towards the end of the year, on the instructions of the GCR, Meyer ordered the contractors to stop work on the Whitton branch until further notice. On the positive side, he was able to say that he had taken steps with regards to the shipment of coal from Winteringham.

The *Stock Exchange Year Book* of 1908 states that the authorised capital of the Company, including loans, was £220,000 of which £78,000 had been issued as Ordinary shares and £30,750 as four per cent Debenture stock.

At first, the union of the GCR and the NLLR Companies was far from smooth and once again a letter from Dixon Davies dated 17 June 1908 to his Board gives a full account:

As part of the campaign with the L&YR last year, we found it necessary to acquire control of the NLLR and subscribed £130,000. The NLLR had, prior to our Agreement, entered into a contract with a construction company called the Leeds Contract Company, formed by their Directors and Officers, for the works from Frodingham to Whitton and the situation between the NLLR Co. and the Leeds Contract Co. has required close investigation in order, not merely to determine the liability of this Company under its Agreement, but to form a scheme by which the NLLR might be put on a firm financial footing.

The Accountant has made several reports. From

74. An RCTS rail tour of 20 June 1954 at West Halton, then the end of the line. The train is headed by ex-GCR class J11 0-6-0 No.64419. *J. W. Armstrong*

these, it will appear that, in several material respects, different views are taken of the pecuniary obligations of the NLLR Co. by the Officers of that Company and by Mr Williams [the GCR Accountant].

Another complexity has arisen from the fact that the contract let by the North Lindsey Company embraced the construction of the line from Winteringham to Whitton which was stopped by the NLLR at the request of the GCR, and a claim arises from the contractors.

The following was put to the North Lindsey Board:
1. The North Lindsey to purchase the land and complete to Whitton.
2. £41,000 was due to the Contractors.
3. All liabilities were to be discharged.
4. The GCR to be given immediately a clear majority on the Board.

My interview with the North Lindsey Solicitor took place to-day, with Sir Berkeley Sheffield and the other Directors, Mr Sisterson of the Leeds Contract Company and Mr Meyer. All parties representing the NLLR wanted costs of the fight with the L&YR. They said it was at the instance of the GCR and on the understanding the GCR would pay the costs. Their

solicitor said roughly £800 to £900. The GCR agreed to pay £13,000 to include the extensions to Alkborough and Barton. This was strongly contested by the North Lindsey people and, for reasons which it would be tedious to go into here, I think there is certainly a great deal to be said on both sides as to this point. I feel very confident that such a settlement is to be recommended in the best interest of the Company. The situation has changed a good deal since the Agreement was entered into and it is not possible to say exactly what the rights of the parties are in the modified circumstances but, if matters were to drift into litigation, there is plenty of room for an uncertain and costly arbitration.

A month later the GCR minuted that the North Lindsey Board had refused to allow the GCR to nominate a majority of Directors to their Board and had appointed Mr Gordon, an Accountant of Leeds, as their Arbitrator. The GCR requested Mr Dunnell, the Solicitor of the NER to act for them. The first duty of the Arbitrators was to select an umpire.

Common sense prevailed and the Terms of an Agreement were signed on 13 August 1908 by S. W.

Meyer, as Director of the North Lindsey, by Edward Sisterson, Director of the Leeds Contract Co. and by D. H. Davies, Solicitor of the GCR. This was to the effect that the GCR paid £50,000 for the whole of the preference capital of the NLLR. The line was to be completed to Whitton according to the conditions of the Agreement of 8 February 1907. The GCR would make a further payment of £5,000 and that sum would be paid in cash to the contractors. Payment in shares would be taken by them for work already done. This, the GCR's final subscription, was subject to there being no further liability.

Following this, the North Lindsey Board agreed to proceed with the Whitton branch. At the same time Philip Meyer resigned from the Board. The GCR nominated Edward (later Sir Edward) Fraser, R. N. Sutton Nelthorpe and W. B. Gair as Directors and W. P. Viccars was elected in place of P. R. Meyer. Plans for the installation of a Riggs Automatic Tippler and for raising the wharf at Winteringham Haven were referred to the GCR.

Messrs Day & Yewdall were instructed by the Company to petition against the Trent Railway & Bridge Company, a company which foundered like the earlier L&YR scheme, by attempting to cross the Lower Trent by means of a bridge. Early in the year R. Burke resigned from the Board. In June the Leeds Contract Co. successfully tendered to build a siding at Frodingham.

The *Doncaster Gazette* reported in 1909 that a workable seam of coal had been discovered at Crosby, near Scunthorpe and that work on a colliery would commence at once on a site as near as possible to the NLLR. In fact a borehole had been sunk and the coal measures reached. But in spite of what the paper has said, it was not commercially practical and no more was heard of the project. Towards the end of the year work commenced on the line to Whitton.

An Amendment Order to the Light Railway Order of 1906 for an Extension of Time was deposited in March 1910. This was considered by the Commissioners in November. They decided

75. Crosby Mines looking south from the road bridge. The line to the right belonged to British Steel. 13 August 1972. *M. A. King*

76. Crosby Mines signal box looking north. The bridge is the A1077 Scunthorpe to Barton-on-Humber road. 13 August 1972. *M. A. King*

that a further public inquiry was unnecessary and the Order was confirmed by the Board of Trade on 17 May 1911.

A contract at £1,534 15s 6d was awarded to Mr H. E. Buckley for doubling the line to Crosby Mines Signal Box and further widening as far as Normanby Park North was decided upon. There was an Agreement in June 1910 between the Leeds Contract Co. and the GCR to rent a building of corrugated iron and wood at Scunthorpe, to be used as an engine shed at £20 per annum.

The extension to Whitton was passed by the Board of Trade inspector for passenger traffic on 7 July and it was opened on 1 December 1910 for goods and passengers. The *Railway Times* reported 'it has been furnished with a nice commodious passenger station adjoining Whitton Ferry on the River Ouse (*sic*) where the daily packet boats from Goole and Gainsborough to Hull will call on their outward and inward journeys'.

Sir Berkeley Sheffield was elected Chairman of the North Lindsey Board in March 1911. It would not be unfair to say that Philip Meyer was dismissed

as Secretary. He was offered £50 as 'Compensation for disturbance on his handing over of documents', or he would be given three months notice. Wisely he accepted the former from 23 March. O. S. Holt, Secretary of the GCR, was appointed in his place at a salary of £25 per annum.

In November the local paper suggested that a start was to be made on the construction of the Barton branch. A new integrated iron and steel plant was erected at Normanby Park by John Lysaght Ltd from 1911 onwards. It was linked to the NLLR by a one-mile branch running north west from the south end of Normanby Park Exchange Sidings. Over the years it provided a significant tonnage to the NLLR.

A year later a further Amendment Order was deposited. This was for a northwards deviation of the line to Barton authorised in 1906. This line was slightly shorter (and cheaper) and it now made an end-on junction with the GCR in that town. The Engineer was F. H. Shipton, a surprising choice as he had been Engineer to the rival and abortive Ackworth & Lindsey and Barton Light Railway

77. Weigh Office Sidings. *M. A. King*

schemes. At least he was familiar with the area.

In December a placard was exhibited at Winteringham Haven:

> HARBOUR DUES payable to
> the North Lindsey Light Railways.
>
> Every vessel loaded with coal, one mete *[appears to be an alternative for one 'Measure']* or two bags of coal. Lime, one mete or two scuttles of lime.
>
> Passengers or other cargo, Fourpence.
>
> PAYABLE to the Station Master at Winteringham.

The public inquiry into the deviation was held in the Assembly Rooms, Barton in February 1913. It was generally agreed that the new plan was an improvement and, indeed, had been recommended by the Commissioners in 1906. The Order was confirmed on 18 June. At the end of the year the papers again prematurely announced that operations were about to be commenced at both ends on the extension.

In 1914 the Treasury refused to make a grant from the Development Fund for the construction of the Winteringham–Barton line, and a Light Railway Order was not approved. In the following year there appears to have been a complete change of heart. By the North Lindsey Light Railways Order of 15 June 1915 the Treasury was to lend £60,000, under the Development and Roads Improvement Fund Act of 1909, to Lindsey County Council, which the Council would lend to the GCR. The North Lindsey could raise a further £93,333 6s 8d, of which the GCR could subscribe £60,000. It seems a very roundabout transaction. Once more it was said that the extension would be commenced.

The North Lindsey Board in 1918 approved the payment of £500 to Sebastian Meyer in full discharge of all sums due to him for engineering services in connection with the extension authorised in 1906.

It is now time to consider the fortunes, or lack of fortune, of the Leeds Contract Company. D.S. Hartmann as 'late Secretary of the Company' wrote, still from 13 Bond Street, Leeds, to the Board of Trade on 24 May 1918: 'The Company has ceased to carry on business as from 31 December 1917, the shareholders having decided not to undertake any further contracts of work. I will try and get in touch with the sole surviving Director of the late Company on the matter, if desired'. This presumably would be Edward Sisterson. A week later Hartmann wrote again; 'The Company has no liabilities and the assets are so small in amount which it is proposed to distribute *pro rata* to the shareholders. It is not necessary to appoint a liquidator and I ask your department to strike this Company off the register'. The Company was dissolved on 18 July 1919.

Returning to the North Lindsey, the *Stock Exchange Year Book* reported in 1920, in the last years of the Company's separate existence, that the Directors were Sir Berkeley Sheffield (Chairman), the Hon. N. Butler-Henderson, Major G. Dove, Sir E. H. Fraser, W. B. Gair, S. W. Meyer and R. Sutton Nelthorpe, of whom the GCR appointed three, although five were obviously GCR nominees. The Secretary was now J. A. Campbell and the offices were at Marylebone. The last Directors, in 1923, were the same except Lord Farringdon replaced Sir Edward Fraser, who had died.

When the Company was taken over by the LNER the shareholders received £102 in cash for each £100 of 4½ per cent Debenture stock, £83 on each £100 of 4 per cent Preference stock, and £80 for each £100 of Ordinary shares. The dividends between 1912 and 1921 had ranged between 3½ and 2½ per cent. £198,374 in shares held by the GCR were cancelled.

The passenger services between Scunthorpe and Whitton ceased on 13 July 1925. Goods traffic beyond West Halton ended officially on 1 October 1951, although it may have ceased before that. Winterton & Thealby to West Halton closed for goods on 29 May 1961. Winterton & Thealby station closed to goods traffic on 20 July 1964.

An unexpected development took place in 1938 and, although it was not a Meyer project, it had such an important effect on the NLLR that it merits mention here. Messrs Lysaghts built a quay on the Trent at Flixborough and linked it to the Normanby Park Works' rail network by a private

78. Weigh Office Sidings signal box taken on the same day as the Crosby Mines photos. *M. A. King*

79. Dawes Lane signal box with Lysaght's steel plant in the background,
13 August 1972. *M. A. King*

single line some two miles long. The works are over 150 feet higher than the wharf, resulting in a gruelling 1 in 40 gradient as the line climbs the escarpment. At a later date a more easily graded line was opened some half mile to the north.

The wharf and railway were opened in May 1938 and the first steamer left on the 13th with a cargo of semi-finished steel for Newport. The Company found this method of transport cheaper than overland carriage. In December, foreshadowing the shape of things to come, 1,000 tons of Swedish steel were landed. The Company used the wharf to transport part-rolled steel from Normanby Park by coaster to its Newport plant in South Wales for finishing there. Flixborough was also used for importing raw materials, principally ferro-alloys from Europe, for steel making at Normanby Park.

The line to Flixborough wharf is still open. Following nationalisation of the three large integrated plants in Scunthorpe in 1967, the British Steel Corporation took over operation of the line from 'Lysaghts' to the wharf. Its function was now extended to include the export of steel to the Con-

tinent, not only from BSC's Scunthorpe plants but also those in the South Yorkshire area, principally Rotherham.

A further, novel development at this stage was the transfer of molten iron (so-called 'hot-metal') in special railborne torpedo vessels between Normanby Park and Appleby-Frodingham Works to make good production imbalances. These torpedo trains were hauled by BSC locomotives between the two works, running over a short distance of NLLR metals immediately south of Crosby Mines Signal Box.

Following the closure of Normanby Park Works, British Railways took over the working of the Flixborough Spur from Normanby Park Exchange Sidings from 11 December 1983. The wharf is now privately operated and traffic over the extant part of the NLLR and Flixborough Spur is greatly diminished.

The North Lindsey Light Railway (Amendment No.2) Order of 12 October 1967 authorised the taking over of the line from Normanby Park North to Winterton & Thealby from British Railways by Richard Thomas & Baldwin Ltd. This firm worked open cast ironstone at the northern end of the NLLR, using its running powers over the line to take the ore to Redbourne Works, Scunthorpe. The Order also authorised the construction of a new line, 396 yards long, from the exchange sidings south of Winterton, curving in a westerly direction, with a new level crossing over the B1430. At the end of the new railway Richard Thomas & Baldwin built an ore loading terminal. The firm closed the NLLR north of the divergence of the new line and engaged in open-cast working on the site of the former trackbed. Open-cast mining in the area has now ceased, resulting in the closure of the railways north of Normanby Park Exchange Sidings.

As the NLLR ran parallel to the lower reaches of the Trent and to the west of the low escarpment, its course was fairly level. The line was double from Trent Junction to Normanby Park North, but is now single. The remainder was single, controlled by Electric Train Staff, to Winterton & Thealby. From there to end of the line was 'one engine in steam' working. Passenger trains had to set back from Winteringham Station and then draw forward to continue to Whitton.

There were signal boxes at Dawes Lane, Weigh Office Sidings, Crosby Mines, Normanby Park South and Normanby Park North. When blasting occurred at the Midland Ironstone's Crosby Mines, all traffic on the NLLR within 200 yards of the blasting between Crosby Mines and Normanby South boxes had to cease. Level crossings were placed at Dawes Lane, Winterton & Thealby, West Halton and near Winteringham.

Although not in use at the present time a line has been retained as far as Roxby Sidings.

CHAPTER ELEVEN

Business activities

MEYER had been associated with Isaac White since 1883 in their work for the E&WYUR and, in particular, since 1896 in the promotion of the Newmarket Branch of that railway to Royds Green Lower. Meyer, White and Ben Day were also involved at about the same time with the CW&SR. White in 1898 leased Spencer Colliery, situated at Royds Green Upper, from J. & J. Charlesworth for £2,776. He was additionally to pay them £200 per annum and 3d per ton of coal for carriage on their tramway. Use of this was in common with the Charlesworths from their collieries down to the Methley Joint line and to the staith on the River Calder. Charlesworths were to have precedence for their own traffic, as they had constructed the tramway down to the river under a lease granted as early as 1838.

Charlesworths had leased the pit to White as they had no immediate use for it except for ventilation, but White had to surrender the pit shaft to them after ten years if required. White at once floated the concern as the Newmarket Haigh Moor Colliery Company with a capital of £10,000 'to work the Spencer and Swithen's pits under licence from the late J.S. Calverley'. The original shareholders included I. White, J. Charlesworth and Ben Day. In 1901 the Directors were Walter Hargreaves (son of William Hargreaves), Ben Day and Sebastian Meyer, now styling himself 'Railway Engineer'. By this time White had died and Meyer may have purchased his shares. This was his first commercial venture apart from his railway activities. The capital of the Company in 1903 was £15,000 and Meyer held 1,140 shares.

Charlesworths gave notice in 1905 that they would end the agreement and require the termination of the lease. In the following year they sold Spencer Pit to Captain Calverley, the ground landlord for £3,000 and ceased paying him £200 a year (presumably the £200 which Haigh Moor were paying them) and they granted Calverley the use of the tramway to the Methley joint line and to the river, again with the proviso that their traffic had preference. Captain Calverley had threatened not to extend the lease to them unless they agreed his conditions. He then leased the Beeston Seam to the Newmarket Haigh Moor Co., who in turn sold their interests to Messrs H. Briggs, Son & Co. Ltd, of Castleford, who intended to sink down to the Silkstone Seam. After this Meyer had no further interest in the colliery, but later developments, as has been seen (Chapter 3) very greatly affected the E&WYUR Co.

With Meyer it would seem that no sooner had he finished with one project, than he must take up another in its place. His next interest was Oleine Ltd. This company was in existence before 1908 but the author has been unable to discover much about it except that it went into voluntary liquidation, the final meeting taking place in February 1909. Meyer was one of its Directors.

A new company was formed in 1908, with a capital of £5,000 and a factory at Ouzelwell Green (situated between Leeds and Wakefield) on land leased from the E&WYUR Co. Its purpose was to extract oils and fats from wool, shoddy, etc; to distil tar; and to manufacture dyes. Oleine itself was used in the cloth industry and was made from raw materials mainly imported through Hull. The Directors were S. W. Meyer, D. S. Hartmann (civil engineer), William McDonnell Mackay (analytical chemist) of Leeds, and J. K. Dixon (chemist) who was to take over as Manager. W. H. Wilson (railway traffic manager) was a shareholder, with probably only a nominal holding. Meyer himself held more than ninety per cent of the shares.

In 1910 Mackay resigned and his place on the Board was taken by Philip John Meyer, Sebastian's elder son. C. W. Walker-Tisdale held 300 shares in 1913. He was closely associated with the Wensleydale Pure Milk Society. During the 1914–1918 war Sebastian Meyer refused to sell any of his products to the Government as he objected to their use for war purposes. Philip Meyer resigned as Director and Manager in 1917 to become Treasurer of the Friends' War Victims' Relief Committee with the tragic result already described (p.34).

Wartime difficulties led to the Debenture holders making an application to the King's Bench Division in 1918. The Company again went into voluntary liquidation but was re-constituted as Oleine Ltd (1920). The final meeting of the old Company was held on 26 June 1922.

The new Company with a capital of £50,000 was formed to acquire as a going concern Oleine Ltd. and the Yorkshire Grease & Fertiliser Co. and to act as oil distillers, tar distillers, manufacturers of manures, dyes and disinfectants – quite a comprehensive list. The Secretary was Sebastian Burtt Meyer (Sebastian's second son), replacing Hartmann who had resigned in 1919. The Registered Office was 13 Bond Street, Leeds. Shareholders included Sebastian W. Meyer, Philip R. Meyer, S. B. Meyer, Mrs Grace Meyer, Miss Ellen Grace Meyer, C. W. Walker-Tisdale and T. C. Mander (former Secretary of the E&WYUR but now described as an estate agent of Uxbridge Road, London). The Company was very soon again in difficulties and Meyer, at the end of 1924, had to obtain an Order for a Receiver, L.D. Kidson being appointed. Voluntary winding up was decided. 'The Company, by reason of its liabilities cannot continue in business'. The Company was formally dissolved on 26 March 1929. The factory was taken over by R.H. Crosby Ltd., of Huddersfield. The building stood until the late 1970s.

Meyer was interested in yet another field. This was the Wensleydale Pure Milk Society. It was formed as a Limited Company in February 1905

and was one of the first in the country to pasteurise milk and distribute it in quart bottles. The promoters were Canon Moore Ede of Sunderland, Arnold Rowntree, Philip Burtt (Deputy General Manager of the North Eastern Railway), Dr Ethel Williams, Dr W. Moore Ede and Mrs Ella Price. The dairy was situated at Northallerton, alongside the NER main line on land leased from that Railway and with its own loading platform. It came into production in October 1905. Milk was collected from Hawes, Askrigg, Aysgarth, Redmire, Leyburn and Sessay. The cows were inspected by the Society's own veterinary surgeons. At first only Newcastle was supplied, but later the milk went to Sunderland, West Hartlepool, Scarborough and London. The first Manager was A.S. Thompson, who had been trained in Denmark.

By 1906 Meyer was Chairman of the Society, a position he held until the end of its existence. The Society soon got into difficulties. Early in 1908 it wrote to the NER asking for a reduction in rates and got a very dusty answer:

'The North Eastern Railway Company is unable to agree to the proposition. Another large company [this refers to a rival milk factory in nearby Nidderdale, mainly supplying Leeds] has worked up its business and they would expect similar terms. The inference one naturally draws is that, if you are failing to carry out your business profitably, which it is not, the reason is to be found, not in the incidence of the rate, but in the management'.

A few months later Dr Moore Ede wrote:

'The Company has been steadily losing money and its affairs had reached a stage when, if they were to be able to carry on their business, some relief would have to be afforded. The farmers were accepting 7d per gallon instead of 7½d. They asked the Railway Company to give further relief of £350 per annum thus enabling them to save, in all, £1,000 per annum without which we are not likely to be able to keep going.'

The NER noted:

The revenue we receive from the Wensleydale Pure Milk Society is considerable and, from comparatively small beginnings, it had risen to nearly £1,200 in 1906 to upwards of £1,800 in 1907. It is suggested that, in view of the magnitude of the business done, we might enter into a new Agreement as in Dr Moore Ede's proposition.

As the NER had second thoughts, the fortunes of

the Society revived and in 1908 the NER provided a special milk-van, No. 125 (LNER No.25Y, later 2125) lettered 'Wensleydale Pure Milk Society Ltd – Northallerton', for its exclusive use.

Success faded away and in 1932 there was a court action brought by C. M. Jenkin Jones, as Manager of the LNER, resulting in that Company taking over the assets of the Society. L. D. Kidson was again appointed Receiver. The Society, by this time including 'The Dairy' at Northallerton, 'The Dairy' at Redmire and 'The Dairy' at West Burton, was sold by auction 'as a going concern' for £8,250. For some reason there was secrecy over the name of the purchasers, but it was generally guessed that it was the Cow & Gate Company of Guildford. The undertaking was transferred to Northern Dairies but the main dairy at Northallerton is now a food factory under another management. The milk platform is still there in a sorry state, but today there is no milk traffic by rail from Northallerton.

A later Managing Director of the Pure Milk Society was C. W. Walker-Tisdale who was an expert in commercial dairying. He wrote a treatise on 'Practical Cheese Making', published by Headley Brothers of London and Ashford. Not surprisingly Meyer was also a Director of this firm.

CHAPTER TWELVE

Civic affairs

SEBASTIAN MEYER was elected in 1902 to York City Council, as a Liberal, representing Bootham Ward. Three years later, at the next election, the papers forecast that he would have a 'walk-over'. For the year 1906–7 he was Sheriff of York and, on retiring, he was made an Alderman and Justice of the Peace.

He was very much a committee-man. He was appointed a member of the Ouse & Foss Navigation Committee in 1906 and, in the following year, he became Vice-Chairman of the Tramways Committee, taking a prominent part in the opening ceremony of York's first electric tramway, from the City to Fulford in 1910. He was Chairman of the Electricity Committee from 1907, of the Waterworks Committee from 1910, of the combined Electricity and Tramways Committee from 1911, Vice-Chairman of the Gas Committee in 1912 and Chairman in the next year.

In 1913, he was offered the office of Lord Mayor but he wrote to the Town Clerk that he was unable to accept the honour, owing to the state of his wife's health.

After World War I, he was involved in the Linton Lock electricity scheme and it was largely through him that York acquired this extra source of power, adding some ten per cent extra to its supplies. The station was a little unusual in that it derived its power from the comparatively slow-moving River Ouse. Meyer visited the site in 1920,

when he made the first concrete block and was presented with a photograph framed in silver of the weir and fish-pass.

In July 1920, after he had left York, Meyer resigned from the City Council, with some suddenness. He sent the Town Clerk a letter enclosing a cheque for £25, which he said was the fine for such resignation. The fine, very properly, was remitted.

On his retirement, the *Yorkshire Gazette* had this to say :

Alderman Meyer, who is a Liberal, has done magnificent work for the City and has been a member of the Council since 1902, when he was elected for Bootham Ward. This he continued to represent until 1907, when he was made an Alderman. He was essentially a committee-man and since the Corporation Tramway system was first established, he has been Chairman of the Electricity and Tramways Committee and it is literally true to say, that he has been the heart of the Committee. Certainly no one has done more for the tramways and it was largely due to him that the City got the Linton Lock scheme.

It would appear that his work for his adopted City was appreciated.

Linton Lock Power House was ceremonially opened by Viscount Lascelles, accompanied by Princess Mary, on 1 August 1923 but it was noticeable that Sebastian Meyer was not present. The station, after nationalisation, was closed down about 1962.

CHAPTER THIRTEEN

Three abortive schemes

AFTER A LULL in his railway promotions, Meyer came up with three new schemes in the period immediately before World War I. None of these railways was built, presumably because of the outbreak of war and the development of road transport afterwards.

The **Brandsby Light Railway** was first proposed in 1911. The promoters were H. C. F. Cholmeley and Oscar Frederic Rowntree, both of Brandsby, and T. C. Horner, a York merchant. The Solicitor to the Company was H. W. Badger, of York. The plans and estimates were signed by Meyer, now styling himself Engineer.

The line was to have run from 150 yards north of Haxby Station, on the York to Scarborough branch of the NER, through Sutton-on-the-Forest and Stillington to Brandsby, just over nine miles. It was to be standard gauge single track, and the motive power steam, or as otherwise approved by the Board of Trade, but not electric. The estimated cost was £33,941 15s and the proposed authorised capital was to be £36,000 with borrowing powers of £12,000. Agreements would be made with the NER for working the line.

The *Railway Times* of 2 December 1911 reported, not entirely accurately:

Road Motor Service precedes a Light Railway. A few years ago the North Eastern Railway Company instituted a road service for the transport of farm produce and heavy goods from Tollerton to Brandsby. This service has given such an impetus to trade of the locality that the Company intend to apply to the Light Railway Commissioners at the next Session for sanction to allow them to construct a Light Railway from Haxby to Brandsby, about ten miles length.

This 'Road Motor Service' was started by the NER in 1904 and ran from Tollerton, on the main line, to Brandsby. Although the word 'motor' was used, it was in fact a steam wagon. Early writers did not think it important to distinguish between steam and petrol vehicles. The original wagon was probably a 'Straker' with solid tyres. The reason for this service was to provide facilities for the Brandsby Dairy Association, whose trade was expanding at that time

The Easingwold Railway Company complained that their returns were being adversely affected, so an arrangement was made in 1906 whereby the NER agreed to transfer the starting point of the route to Easingwold so that the smaller company obtained its share of the traffic. The Easingwold Company built a corrugated iron garage at Easingwold Station to house the NER lorry.

In spite of the *Railway Times* optimism, the farmers' traffic did not develop as expected, the trade of the dairy did not continue to expand as hoped and the steam wagons proved expensive and unreliable in use, although the service continued until 1915.

There was a public inquiry before the Light Railway Commissioners in York on 21 February 1912. The *Yorkshire Herald* reported:

There was no serious opposition, except from the Easingwold Railway. At Brandsby, there was an agricultural co-operative society which, owing to the foresight of the NER, had been in touch with Easingwold by means of a motor wagon but that is a very unsatisfactory way of getting produce from one place to another and it is quite uncertain whether that service would be continued. It did not carry passengers.

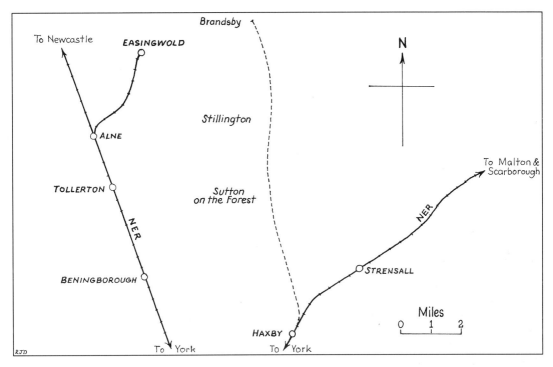

80. The Proposed Brandsby Light Railway.

The Co-operative had practically guaranteed 3,200 tons of freight per annum if the railway were carried through. The village would develop as a residential area. There were no engineering difficulties. Alderman Sebastian Meyer gave evidence, saying that he had considerable experience in constructing Light Railways including the Selby & Cawood, the Isle of Axholme and several other lines. The plans had been made under his supervision. The line was nearly level, with a gradient of 1 in 100 for 1¾ miles and another short distance of 1 in 50 which would be close to Brandsby. There were no cuttings: it was a surface line with level crossings and a few drains to cross. The River Foss was practically a drain. There would be three stations and two halts, the former at Sutton, Stillington and Brandsby. It would be worked by 'one engine in steam' and practically without signals. He estimated the cost at £33,941, the earnings at £5,200 with expenses at £2,700 per annum. On a capital of £36,000 with £12,000 on Debentures, 4 per cent on the Debentures and 5 per cent on the Ordinary shares would come to £2,280 which would leave a small balance. He thought the line would not compete with the Easingwold Railway. 'If I thought the line would injure the Easingwold, I should not have been here to-day'.

Councillor O. Rowntree thought the motor service was quite inadequate besides being inconvenient. Mr Fairfax Cholmeley, who had extensive estates at Brandsby, said the proposed extension of the Easingwold Railway was too roundabout and that the principal object of the new scheme was not merely to serve the interests of the Co-operative.

Henry Maxted, Secretary and General Manager of the Co-operative, said the industry of the district had been hampered by the lack of facilities in carriage. His Society would provide 3,000 tons per annum and it would be the largest customer as it was a combination of farmers. The motor at present carried about 2,000 tons per annum of the Society's goods.

The scheme was opposed by the Easingwold Railway who admitted that the present conditions were not all that could be desired but the Company would cease to pay if the Light Railway were sanctioned. The only big customer was the Co-operative. It had considered last November an extension to Stillington and Farlington which would meet the needs of the district.

Dr Edward Hicks, Secretary of the Easingwold Railway and a local General Practitioner, said the Company had only kept out of the Bankruptcy Court with difficulty and they would not have done so without the consideration of the NER. There was now a regularly established motor wagon system. His Company had discussed the extension to Sherrif Hutton and that would be a better proposal but it would not extend to Brandsby.

The Chairman said the Commissioners were in favour of granting the Order and they thought the Section of the Act quoted on competition was not intended to refer to the present conditions. (The Board of Trade could reject any application because of its effect on an existing railway).

The Order was submitted to the Board of Trade on 29 April 1912 but the reference was suspended pending an application to the Development Commissioners for financial assistance. In August of the following year the *Railway Times* reported that the Promoters of the Brandsby Light Railway had been informed by the Development Commissioners that

the Treasury had agreed to make a grant of £20,000 from the Development Fund towards the construction of thirteen (*sic*) miles of Light Railway from Haxby to Brandsby, serving a rich agricultural area. Application was being made to the County Council for a loan of £5,000.

In spite of all this, nothing further is heard of the proposal after this date.

Contemporary with these events a similar scheme was being put forward in the northern part of the County. This was the **Swaledale Light Railway**, promoted by James W. Close, whose name has already been mentioned several times, and Sebastian Burtt Meyer, Sebastian's second son. The Solicitors were Scratchard, Hopkins & Co of Leeds and the plans and estimates were signed by Sebastian William Meyer in November 1911. The proposed line was ten miles long, from a junction with the NER, east of Richmond Station, along Swaledale, to terminate near Grinton Bridge on the road from Grinton to Reeth. The estimated cost was £40,307 10s and the authorised capital was

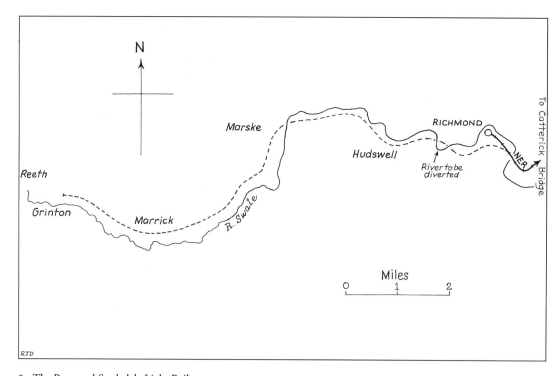

81. The Proposed Swaledale Light Railway.

to be £42,000 with borrowing powers of £12,000. It was standard gauge, single track and the motive power was not to be electric. There would be two stations and three halts. It was agreed that the line would be worked in perpetuity by the NER.

A public inquiry was held in Richmond on 22 February 1912 before the Light Railway Commissioners. It was reported that there was little or no opposition. There would be no viaducts (but it was not explained how the River Swale was to be crossed), embankments, gatehouses or level crossings. The line would help the chert and lead mines. Chert is a valuable silica mineral used in the pottery industry. It was also expected that there would be a heavy holiday passenger traffic.

J. W. Close, originally a native of Low Whitta, a small hamlet a few miles west of Grinton, and owner of 500 acres of land in the Dale, said that fifty years ago there was a large lead industry in the district but, owing to the heavy cost of carriage, this had stopped.

Alderman S. W. Meyer of York said he had considerable experience of light railway construction. He estimated the receipts at £4,200 a year and expenses at £3,000, which he said would leave £1,200 for emergencies. The promoters had been in communication with the Treasury who were authorised to subscribe public money for schemes of this sort if it were proved to the satisfaction of the Board of Agriculture that the scheme would be of benefit to the district.

The Board had issued their Certificate that the railway was desirable. Application had been made to Reeth Rural District Council that they should lend £10,000 to the Company, but they had not agreed. They intended to continue negotiations with the Council. There would be stations at Marske and Grinton and halts at Hudswell and Marrick, with sidings at the stations for use by the farmers. The worst gradient was 1 in 50 and the sharpest curve one of 10 chains. The line would rise gradually and would be nearly 200 feet above the level of its commencement.

Mr Dunnell, Solicitor of the NER, said his Company did not approve of the proposed site of the junction at Richmond. The space was limited. He was, however, prepared to let the Order go forward in its present form, but he had to tell the Commissioners he did not favourably view the present junction.

The Commissioners were satisfied that the Light Railway would be of great benefit to the farmers and, subject to the financial arrangements, which Mr Meyer had spoken of, being shown to their satisfaction, they were prepared to let the Order through. They thought it desirable that the Local Authorities who had been in negotiation with the promoters should, in view of Treasury assistance, be prepared to some extent to put their hands in their pockets.

By April 1912 the engineers reported that they had nearly completed their measurements on the proposed alterations at the junction. Mr Close reported in March 1913 'the whole thing has been thrashed out' at a meeting in York. It was stated in April 1913 that a start was to be made on the construction of the Swaledale Railway and, again, in November that an early start would be made and that tenders would shortly be asked for. In May of that year the Treasury conditionally promised a loan.

There was, however, some opposition necessitating a further application to the Light Railway Commissioners. As stated the NER did not approve the junction with their line at Richmond and the plans were altered so that the Light Railway passed behind some cottages near the station instead of in front of them, and joined the NER a few yards further east. One landowner objected and the Swale was now to be crossed a little to the west of the original site.

In December 1914 the Commissioners intimated to the Richmond Rural District Council that the amended Order, passed by them, had been submitted to the Board of Trade for confirmation. Nothing further on the proposal has been traced.

The last railway promotion with which Meyer was associated was the **Hutton Magna Light Railway** which was more successful than the other two schemes in that it managed to obtain its Light Railway Order from the Board of Trade. The end result however was the same. It too faded away. It was promoted in 1913 by William Spencer, a quarry owner and limestone merchant of Keighley. The Solicitors were Spencer, Clarkson & Co of Keighley and the Engineer was Sebastian William Meyer. The 3½ mile railway was to run from a junction with the Forcett Railway (a nominally

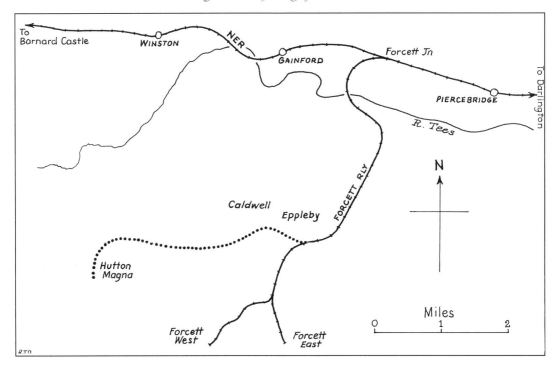

82. The Proposed Hutton Magna Light Railway.

independent line worked by the NER as a branch from their Darlington–Barnard Castle line) near the village of Eppleby to quarries near the village of Hutton Magna. The purpose was to reach the extensive limestone deposits and carry them for use by the iron smelting industry of Teesside. It would also serve the agricultural interests of the district.

The estimated cost was £22,356 and the authorised capital would be £24,000 with borrowing powers of £8,000. The gauge was to have been standard, with Agreements with the NER and the Forcett Railway for working and running powers. The motive power was not to be electric. The NER's Solicitor considered that if his Company was to work the line the weight of the rails would have to be carefully examined.

Colonel Boughey, the Light Railway Commissioner, reported that the promoter was William Spencer and the Engineer Sebastian William Meyer 'who is well known to us'. It was not proposed to carry passenger traffic, but it seemed desirable to him that the Light Railway and the Forcett Railway

should be opened for passengers with a possible station near the junction to serve the villages of Caldwell and Eppleby. A public inquiry was held at the King's Head Hotel, Barnard Castle on 14 February 1914. The Light Railway Commissioners approved the Draft Order and it was confirmed by the Board of Trade on 17 May 1915. The requirements for munitions at this time may have had some influence on the decision. But this was never acted upon.

A NOTE ON TREASURY FUNDING

The Treasury could make special advances either by a free grant and/or loan, provided the Board of Agriculture certified that the construction of a light railway would benefit agriculture in the area, or the Board of Trade confirmed that the building of the railway was necessary for the development of the district, but, owing to exceptional circumstances, the railway would not be constructed without financial aid from the Government.

The Treasury also had to be satisfied that an existing operating railway company had agreed, provided that such a grant had been made, to work the light railway. An advance could not be made by the Treasury until they were satisfied that landowners, local authorities and other interested parties had given all possible assistance in their power for the construction of the line. The advance was not to be more than half the estimated cost of the railway.

CHAPTER FOURTEEN

Conclusion

THE names of the same men crop up over and over again in this story, forming a very definite combine, or, less charitably, an 'old boy' network. Perhaps, but for his early death, the most important of these would have been Isaac White. He was one of the first to be associated with Meyer when he, White, was Engineer to the Goole & Marshland, the Isle of Axholme, the Cawood, Wistow & Selby and the South Leeds Junction railways. He held directorships in the Newmarket Haigh Moor Colliery Company, the E&WYUR, the CW&SLR, the SLJR and in the Yorkshire District Light Railway Syndicate.

Edward Sisterson, the iron and steel merchant from Newcastle-on-Tyne, first appeared offering 'slightly defective rails' to the North Sunderland Light Railway. Later he became a Director (and Chairman in 1909) of the NSLR, the E&WYUR, the Brackenhill Light Railway and the NLLR, as well as of the YDLR and the Leeds Contract Company.

Ben Day became Solicitor to the E&WYUR in 1895 and a Director in 1909. His senior partner in the legal firm of Yewdall & Day had joined the Board in 1901 and had become Chairman in 1906, and both Day and Sisterson retained these positions until the 1923 Grouping. Day was also Solicitor to the CW&SLR, the Brackenhill and the DVR.

David Stuart Hartmann was employed by the E&WYUR in 1887 as assistant clerk, but he rapidly rose to the position of Engineer to that Company. He was Temporary Secretary to the CW&SLR in 1896, probably at the same time as he was working for the E&WYUR. He was a director of the Brackenhill. He was Secretary and Director of Oleine Ltd until he resigned in 1919, and Secretary to the

Leeds Contract Company until it was wound up in 1919. He died in Leeds in 1924.

James W. Close was a Director and later Chairman of the Yorkshire Railway Wagon Co. He was Auditor of the CW&SLR, the DVR and the Great Northern Railway and a Director of the Leeds Contract Co. Surprisingly he crops up again in 1911 as promoter of the Swaledale Light Railway.

Lastly there was Philip Robert Meyer, Sebastian's younger brother, who usually appeared in a subsidiary position. He was Auditor to the E&WYUR from 1892 to 1899. He was appointed Traffic Manager to the Goole & Marshland in 1899 and was a Director of the Isle of Axholme. He was Director and Secretary, later Secretary only, of the NLLR, but he was made redundant by the Great Central Railway when that Company took over the Light Railway. He was for a time Director and also Secretary of the Brackenhill Light Railway, which latter position he held until 1923. He retired at first to Harrogate, but afterwards he lived in Richmond, Surrey at the home of his brother Henry. He died in 1933.

Sebastian Meyer very quickly realised the advantages of the Light Railways Act. As already said, the Order for the Newmarket branch of the East & West Yorkshire Union was only the second one to be sanctioned. The Light Railways Act was passed on 14 August 1896 (59&60 Vic.c.48) and as there have been so many references to it a short description follows.

Strangely, the Act gives no definition of a 'Light Railway'. It was generally accepted however that a light railway was one built as cheaply as possible, with the minimum of engineering works and using lightweight rails. Signals were not required except at junctions and passing places. Station platforms need not be provided as long as passengers had means of access to ground level and shelter was not considered necessary. Continuous braking did not have to be provided on passenger trains (although the Board of Trade insisted on it in certain cases). The promoters did not have to fence off the line. It was not necessary to have gates at level crossings, but, in their absence, cattle guards had to be provided. There was a speed limit of 25 miles per hour, reduced to only 10 over level crossings.

The Act authorised the appointment of three Light Railway Commissioners. The first three were the Earl of Jersey, a politician and landowner; Gerald Fitzgerald, a barrister; and Colonel George Boughey of the Royal Engineers. Only the last was paid a salary. The initial public inquiry into an application for a Light Railway Order was held before them and, if approved, it was referred to the Board of Trade for confirmation. The Board (and the Commissioners) could withhold approval of an Order (1) if by reason of the magnitude of the scheme it should be submitted to Parliament; (2) because of its effect upon any existing railway company; or (3) for any special reason relating to the undertaking.

A draft model Order was prepared and if the promoters deviated from this, they had to show very good cause. The Board of Trade could consider any further objections and make alterations to the Order before finally confirming it. Generally a Light Railway Order was much cheaper to obtain than an Act, but the process took longer.

The Light Railways Act was intended to open up rural areas and benefit agriculture and, in certain cases, help small fishing ports. The conditions on which the Treasury could assist have already been described.

All Meyer's railways except the Dearne Valley were built under Light Railway Orders or subsequently obtained one. It is very doubtful if the promoters of the Act intended it to facilitate the construction of mineral lines such as the Newmarket Branch, the Brackenhill or the North Lindsey Light.

After his resignation from the City Council in 1920 and his leaving York, Meyer had many changes of address. Following the Railway Group-ing of 1923 he had no railway activity except his Directorship of the NSLR. He resided for a time in Ilkley and in Burley-in-Wharfedale. For some years he made his home in Ripon, which was convenient for his association with the Wensley-dale Pure Milk Society. At this time he bought a car in order to travel to Northallerton, but never really mastered the art of driving. It was said he was unable to reverse. Perhaps in those days of less crowded roads this did not matter.

About this period, at the age of 70, he started to learn Greek, teaching himself. He questioned the accepted translation of parts of the New Testament and he wanted to make his own. It is said he brought fresh enlightenment to those who were in contact with him. While at Ripon, at the age of 82, he entered the Swaledale Tournament of Song at Rich-mond and won first prize with a composition for the harp, the family tradition coming out once more.

He spent his last years with his surviving son, Sebastian Burtt Meyer, first of all at Bourneville and latterly at Yealand Conyers, near Carnforth. By this time he was in somewhat reduced circum-stances, at least compared with his state of affluence in the early years of the century. It is thought he kept his money invested in railways and coal mines for too long.

He died at Yealand Conyers on 15 July 1946, at the age of 90, and was buried in the Friends' Burial Ground at that place.

After this lapse of time it is difficult to assess the true character of the man. There is no doubt he had very great personal charm and more than his fair share of good looks. He must have been an extrovert; no-one without abundant self-confidence would have styled himself 'Railway Expert' or, without proper training, 'Railway Engineer'. He had an infinite capacity for work and during his career must have travelled many thousands of miles.

He had the reputation of always being willing to help others. He was a man of firm religious beliefs and may be described as a 'pillar of the Church'. He was an entirely self-made man – a typical example of Victorian 'self-help'.

All his railways which were built were, with one exception, taken over sooner or later by main-line companies. It can, therefore, be said that his proposals, at least in their early years, were success-ful. Some of them appear to have operated on a 'happy-go-lucky' system. But no serious accident, except the one during the construction of the Goole & Marshland Railway, has been recorded. His railways, with few exceptions have disappeared, one cannot say without trace, as some remains will still be found as 'Forgotten Railways'.

His other business activities were not so successful, often ending by the calling in of a Receiver. It is said he was too honest, humane and considerate for the business world and his family thought he would be more suited to a Chair of Philosophy.

This book started with a comparison between Meyer and Colonel Stephens, so it can conclude with a description of their railways to-day. Only two of Stephens' lines are now used as part of British Railways, the branch from Bere Alston to Gunnislake and the Burry Port & Gwendraeth. Two are in the hands of preservation societies, and there are proposals to take over a third.

None of Meyer's railways is 'preserved' or likely to be. Several sections are in active use. One which neither Meyer or his associates could ever have imagined is that part of the Dearne Valley which formed the flying junction to join the East Coast Main Line. It was brought back into use in May 1977 in connection with the Doncaster re-signalling, electrified, and now allows trains from the Up side of Doncaster station to reach the Down slow line or the GN&GE Joint line without fouling the fast main lines. It now carries a regular passenger service, which it never did in Meyer's time.

Other parts of the DVR and the North Lindsey Light still carry mineral traffic, although their mileage has been greatly reduced. Coal is carried from Grimethorpe Colliery to the former Midland Main Line by a new connection opened in July 1966 and from Goldthorpe Colliery by another new connection, opened on 14 May 1978, to the Swinton & Knottingley Joint line. In this case coal travels in the opposite direction to that originally envisaged, which was to take coal from Hickleton Main Colliery to the DVR. With the rapid shrinkage of the South Yorkshire Coalfield, one hesitates to predict how long these will last.

The North Lindsey still carries iron and steel traffic, but perhaps not in the form or the direction the promoters of the line expected. It has seen both expansion and contraction in recent years. The line to Flixborough Wharf is now worked by BR, but shunting at the wharf is done by the steel company's locomotives.

It will be seen that some of Meyer's railways are carrying out their original intention, that of conveying mineral traffic and it is probably correct to say that Meyer has made a more lasting impression on the railway map of today than Stephens.

It is fitting to end with part of his obituary notice from *The Friend*, the Journal of The Society of Friends. 'Though his opportunities in youth were limited, his education continued through his long and varied career. In the active middle years of his life he rose to great eminence, taking a leading part in the development of Light Railways in the North of England, and also in the life of the City of York, where he was an active member of the Council and, at one time, held the office of Sheriff. His ministry in the York Meeting is still remembered appreciatively.'

APPENDIX A: Summary of Acts of Parliament and Light Railway Orders

CHAPTER 2
East and West Yorkshire Union Railways Co.

2 August 1883. 46-7 Vic,c.166
Incorporation. Construction powers from Leeds, Ardsley and Lofthouse to Drax.

25 June 1886. 49-50 Vic,c.81
May abandon authorised lines at Ardsley and Lofthouse. Replaced by new lines.

24 July 1888. 51.2 Vic, c.130
Extension of time. Bridge over A&CN to be opening bridge.

26 July 1889. 52-3 Vic, c.94 (GNR Act)
Fly-over Junction at Lofthouse.

12 August 1889. 52-3 Vic, c.121
Short length to be abandoned in Leeds.

25 July 1890. 53-4 Vic, c.127
Main line Leeds to Drax abandoned.

24 August 1893. 56-7 Vic, c.219
South Leeds Junction Railway Act. Incorporation. Construction powers from Rothwell to Stourton.

20 July 1894. 57-8 Vic, c.82
Authorised railway at Ardsley abandoned.

2 July 1896. 59-60 Vic, c.42
East & West Yorkshire Union Railways (South Leeds Junction Railway Transfer) Act. SLJR vested in E&WYUR Co.

14 December 1897. LRO
Construction powers Robin Hood–Royds Green Lower.

1899. Board of Trade Certificate. May raise additional £36,000 capital, with Borrowing Powers of £12,000.

7 June 1901. LRO
Construction powers Stourton–Hunslet. May operate existing railway as Light Railway.

4 November 1907. LRO
Additional Borrowing Powers of £14,000.

CHAPTER 4
North Sunderland Light Railway

27 June 1892. 55-56 Vic, c.155
Incorporation. Construction powers Chathill – Seahouses.

13 August 1898. LRO
Construction powers Seahouses –

Monks House. Railway to be worked as Light Railway.

CHAPTER 5
Cawood, Wistow & Selby Light Railway Company

2 July 1896. 59-60 Vic, c.46
Incorporation; construction powers from Selby to Cawood.

30 July 1900. 63-4 Vic, c.163
(NER Act) Extension in Cawood; purchase by NER.

CHAPTER 6
Dearne Valley Railway Company

6 August 1897. 60-1 Vic, c.243
Incorporation; Construction powers Brierley Junction – Bessacarr Junction, and dock on Sheffield & South Yorkshire Navigation at Mexborough.

30 July 1900. 63-4 Vic, c.126
Extension of time.

26 July 1901. 1 Ed.VII, c.130
L&YR Dearne Valley Junction Railways Act. Construction powers Crofton – Shafton.

31 July 1902. 2 Ed.VII, c.158
(L&YR Act). Powers to subscribe to DVR.

1 August 1904. 4 Ed.VII, c.149
(L&YR Act). Powers to make Agreements with DVR. Construction powers for branch to Denaby Colliery.

30 June 1905. 5 Ed.VII, c.55
Further extension of time and additional capital powers.

20 July 1906. 6 Ed.VII, c.95
(L&YR Act). May subscribe further capital to DVR.

CHAPTER 7
Brackenhill Light Railway Company

19 March 1901. LRO
Incorporation. Construction powers Hemsworth–Ackworth & branches.

22 September 1904. LRO
Extension of Time.

16 April 1907. LRO
Extension of Time.

18 November 1911. 1-2 Geo.V, c.94
(NER Act). Extension of Time.

CHAPTER 8
Axholme Light Railways

16 August 1898. LRO
Incorporation; Goole & Marshland Light Railway. Construction powers Marshland Junction–Fockerby.

11 March 1899. LRO
Incorporation; Isle of Axholme Light Railway. Construction powers Haxey–Reedness Junction and branches.

31 July 1902. 2 Ed.VII, c.168
(NER Act). Purchase of both Light Rlys by NER and L&YR.

5 August 1905. LRO
Axholme Jt Rly (Hatfield Moor Extension). Construction powers Epworth–Hatfield Moor.

16 August 1909. 9 Ed.VII, c.48
(L&Y and NER Act). (Hatfield Moor Further Extension) Construction powers Hatfield Moor–Black Carr.

23 March 1910. LRO
Axholme Jt Rly (Hatfield Moor Extension) Deviation.

15 August 1913. 3-4 Geo.V, c.66
(L&YR Act). Extension of Time for LRO 1905.

10 March 1917. LRO
Axholme Jt Rly (Hatfield Moor Extension). Revival of powers.

28 July 1921. 11.2 Geo.V, c.35
(NER Act). Extension of Time for LRO 1910.

18 July 1923. 13-4 Geo.V, c.28
(LNER Act). Extension of Time for LRO 1910.

1 August 1924. 14-5 Geo.V, c.54
(LMS Act). Extension of Time for LRO 1905 and Act 1909.

29 June 1927. 18-9 Geo.V, c.16
(LMS Act). Extension of Time for LRO 1910.

2 July 1928. 18-9 Geo.V, c.44
(LMS Act). Extension of Time for LRO 1905 and Act 1909.

31 July 1931. 21-2 Geo.V, c.92
(LNER Act). Extension of Time for LRO 1910 to 1 October 1936.

CHAPTER 9
Tickhill Light Railway

7 August 1901. LRO
Incorporation. Construction powers

Tickhill–Bawtry–Haxey.
22 September 1904. LRO
Extension of Time.
4 November 1908. LRO
GNR (Tickhill Light Railway).
Amendment and Transfer Order.
20 July 1922. 12-13 Geo.V, c.J19
(GNR Act). Extension of Time.

CHAPTER 10
North Lindsey Light Railways Company
29 January 1900. LRO
Incorporation. Construction powers

Scunthorpe–Whitton.
20 January 1905. LRO
Amendment Order. Alterations at
Frodingham.
10 July 1906. LRO
Extensions Order.
Whitton–Alkborough and
Winteringham–Barton-on-Humber.
26 July 1907. 7 Ed.VII, c.78
(GCR Act). Lines at Winteringham
Haven.
17 May 1911. LRO
Amendment Order. Extension of
time.

18 June 1913. LRO
Amendment Order. Deviation at
Barton-on-Humber.
15 June 1915. LRO
Amendment Order. Further capital.
12 October 1967. LRO
Amendment Order No.2.

CHAPTER 13
Hutton Magna Light Railway
17 May 1915. LRO
Incorporation. Construction powers,
junction with Forcett Railway to
Hutton Magna.

APPENDIX B: Bibliography

GENERAL

Acts, Deposited Plans and Minutes of the various Railway Companies.
Appendix to Rules and Regulations and to Working Timetables, Southern Area, LNER, 1947
Appendix to Rules and Regulations and to Working Time Tables, North Eastern Area, LNER, 1947
Barnett, A. L., *The Railways of the South Yorkshire Coalfield from 1880*, Railway Correspondence & Travel Society, 1984
Bosley, Peter, *Light Railways in England and Wales*, Manchester University Press, 1990
Clinker, C. R., *Light Railway Orders*, Avon-Anglia, Weston-super-Mare, 1977
Dow, George, *Great Central*, Vol III, Ian Allen, 1965
Hoole, K. (ed), *Hull & Barnsley Railway*, Vol I, David & Charles, Newton Abbot, 1972
Joy, D., *Regional History of the Railways of Great Britain*, Vol 8: *South and West Yorkshire*, David & Charles, Newton Abbot, 1984
Kidner, R. W., *The Light Railways of Britain*, Oakwood Press, Chislehurst, 1947
Kidner, R. W., *Locomotives of the LNER, Part 8B, Tank engines – classes J71 to J94*, Railway Correspondence

& Travel Society, 1971
Mabbott, F. W., *Manning Wardle & Company Ltd Locomotive Works List*, Alexander, Birmingham, 1982
Marshall, John, *The Lancashire & Yorkshire Railway*, Vol II, David & Charles, Newton Abbot, 1970
Morgan, J. S., *The Colonel Stephens Railways*, David & Charles, Newton Abbot, 1978
Simnett, W. E., *Railway Amalgamation in Great Britain*, Railway Gazette, 1923
Sectional Appendix to Working Timetables, Central Division, LMS, 1937
Steward, H. A., *The Light Railways Act*, Eyre & Spottiswood, 1893

REGIONAL

Franks, D. L., *East & West Yorkshire Union Railways*, Turntable, Leeds, 1973
Goode, G. T., *The Dearne Valley Railway*, Goode, Hull, 1986
Hallas, C. S., *The Wensleydale Railway*, Dalesman, Clapham, N. Yorks, 1984
Hoole, K., *North Eastern Railway Buses, Lorries and Autocars*, Nidd Valley Narrow Gauge Railways, Knaresborough, 1969
Hoole, K., *Railways in the Yorkshire

Dales*, Dalesman, Clapham, N. Yorks, 1975
Oates, G., *The Axholme Joint Railway*, Oakwood Press, Lingfield, 1961
Wright, A., *The North Sunderland Railway*, 2nd edn, Oakwood Press, Oxford, 1988

OTHER SOURCES

Bradshaw's Railway Manuals and Timetables
Directory of Directors
Kelly's Directories
Monthly Meeting Minutes (Leeds and York), Society of Friends
Railway Year Books
Register of Defunct Companies
Stock Exchange Year Book
York City Council Minutes
York Directories
Newspapers and Periodicals:
Branch Line News; Colliery Guardian; Doncaster Gazette; Eastern Morning News; Goole Times; Howdenshire Gazette; Hull Times; Lindsey & Lincolnshire Star; The Locomotive; Pontefract Express; Railway Gazette; Railway Magazine; Railway Observer; Railway Times; Selby Express; Wakefield Express; Wakefield Herald; Yorkshire Gazette; Yorkshire Herald; Yorkshire Post.

Index